George Edward Weare

A Collectanea Relating to the Bristol Friars Minors (Gray Friars) and Their Convent

Together with a concise history of the dissolution of the houses of the four orders of mendicant friars in Bristol

George Edward Weare

A Collectanea Relating to the Bristol Friars Minors (Gray Friars) and Their Convent
Together with a concise history of the dissolution of the houses of the four orders of mendicant friars in Bristol

ISBN/EAN: 9783337218904

Printed in Europe, USA, Canada, Australia, Japan

Cover: Foto ©ninafisch / pixelio.de

More available books at **www.hansebooks.com**

A Friar Minor without his Mantle.

A Collectanea

RELATING TO

The Bristol Friars Minors

(GRAY FRIARS)

And their Convent,

TOGETHER WITH

A Concise History of the Dissolution of the Houses of the Four Orders of Mendicant Friars in Bristol,

BY

G. E. WEARE.

BRISTOL:
W. BENNETT, PRINTER, 43, BROAD STREET.

1893.

Preface.

FOR many years it has appeared to me that an effort should be made to rescue from obscurity a little information concerning the Friars Minors of Bristol, and their convent; and on several occasions I have tried to induce competent persons to undertake the task, but without success. It came to my knowledge more than twenty years ago that, notwithstanding statements to the contrary in nearly all Bristol Histories containing references to the Friars, there were some remains of the conventual buildings still in existence, and some old deeds clearly demonstrated that "Blackfriars," the name by which a considerable portion of the Gray Friars inclosure has been known for a long period, was a misnomer. In vain have I attempted to bring the facts before persons in authority, with a view to an alteration of the name which is so conspicuously affixed to walls in the neighbourhood. "The old inhabitant" is sometimes found to be a difficult person to deal with; he has heard some trumped-up story told on many occasions, and by various individuals; and he has probably repeated it so often to others, that he is aghast when he hears a suggestion that his phantom castle stands a chance of being demolished by facts. Only a wicked unbeliever in local traditions would attempt to make war on the imaginary "Blackfriars" of Lewins Mead. In connection with the history of Bristol, it cannot be gainsaid that it is desirable to destroy the false local traditions, some of which, doubtless, possess much to interest, I had almost said to fascinate the reader, and which have been accepted for generations as historic truth; and to substitute for them a well authenticated, but possibly less attractive, and less exciting record of local events. It was only after much hesitation that I resolved to take the subject matter of this little work in hand, and I should not have proceeded with the compilation had I not received kind encouragement and practical help from Mr. John Latimer, who is one of the best living authorities on the history of the city.

I am also indebted for assistance and advice, to Mr. Alderman Fox, Mr. William George, Rev. Father Grant, Mr. Richard Howlett, Mr. G. H. Jeayes, (British Museum); The Rev. C. F. R. Palmer, (St. Dominic's Priory, London); Mr. T. S. Pope (who has kindly supplied the sketches); The Rev. Prebendary Salmon, (Rector of Weston-super-Mare); Mr. John Taylor, Mr. Robert Hall Warren, Miss E. M. Walford, The Rev. T. P. Wadley, the Trustees of the Moravian Chapel (who are the present owners of a substantial portion of the land which originally formed the Friars Inclosure); and Messrs. Brittan, Livett & Miller, their solicitors; the City Treasurer, the Secretary of the Bristol Charity Trustees, and Mr. Goodenough Taylor and his Co-partners, the Proprietors of the *Bristol Times & Mirror.*

I think I may fairly claim that as the result of considerable labour, which has not been carried on without expense, I have been able to bring to light some hitherto unpublished records and entries relating to an obscure portion of local history. It is possible that when the State Papers have been properly catalogued and indexed, a work that will take a considerable number of years to accomplish, some, but probably not much, additional information may be forthcoming.

In conclusion I will ask my readers to deal generously with any shortcomings, errors, or faults which they may discover.

G. E. WEARE.

16, ELLENBOROUGH CRESCENT,
    WESTON-SUPER-MARE,
        January, 1893.

A Friar Minor with his Mantle.

The Friars Minors,

or

Gray Friars.

Introductory.

THE founder of the Order was Francis, the son of a rich merchant named Pietro Bernadone and Madonna Pica his wife, of Assissi (in Italy), at which place he was born in or about A.D. 1182. He died on the 4th day of October, A.D. 1226, which day was appointed as "The Festival of St. Francis," when he was canonized by Pope Gregory IX.

It was in or about the year 1206 that the founder of the order became strongly affected with religious zeal, and made a resolution to retire from the world, and this year has been assigned by some writers as the date of the commencement of the order. Wadding, the English Franciscan Annalist, (whose work is contained in 20 MS. folio volumes) puts the date, A.D. 1207, and A.D. 1209 has also been given.

These discrepancies may easily be accounted for in consequence of the Pope's reluctance to recognize in an official form the work of the founder. Mr. Richard Howlett, of the Middle Temple, in his well-constructed and learned preface to vol. II. of Monumenta Franciscana (Rolls series) p. 9, says, " Whatever the reason for reluctant action may "have been, it was certainly only after much hesitation " that in 1209, St. Francis was accorded verbally the " approbation of the Pope. No Bull or writing was given, " nay, distinctly refused, and a way for the suppression of " the new movement, should it be found practically in- " convenient, was then visibly left open for some years, " until, in 1215, it was judged that the Order of St. Francis " might be put upon a permanent footing; even then the " rule was only approved verbally by the Lateran Council. " More, perhaps, could hardly be expected from an assembly " which was enacting a decree against the origination of " new religious orders, but this is in itself good witness " to the early merits of the Franciscans."

The founder held his first general chapter in or about A.D. 1216, and "he then sent out many of his Friars to " preach by both example and word, and had the comfort " to hear that his and their labours were blessed with a " great conversion of sinners to true penance, and much " increase of fervour in religion and devotion, and that the " number of his followers multiplied almost daily."— (Collectanea Anglo-Minoritica, p. 5).

In the year 1219, St. Francis convened a second general chapter at the little Church of the Portiuncula, near Assisi, given to him by the Benedictine Monks of Monte Subiaco, and which, with the grounds adjoining, constituted the first Franciscan Convent. It is recorded that at this celebrated Chapter there were no less than 5,000 Friars assembled in the fields adjoining the Church. This gathering has been designated the "Chapter Storearum"—the assembly of the Straw Huts—so called from the materials used in the formation of the temporary shelters for the assembled Friars. It was at this general Chapter that St. Francis resolved to extend his mission throughout the world.

The order was officially recognised by the Pope by a Bull, dated the 29th day of November, 1223.

. . . .

The Friars were designated "Franciscans" from the name of the founder; they were in general, and in nearly all legal and other writings styled Friars Minors, from Frati Minori, or Fratres Minores, (inferior or minor brothers) which was the title given them by by St. Francis; they were not unfrequently called "Minorites," and Minorite Convent was often applied as the description of a Franciscan house. They were distinguished from the three other orders of Mendicant Friars in England by the colour of their habit, which consisted of a long gray coat down to the heels, with a cowl or hood of the same colour, hence "Grayfriars." Gray was generally the colour used in the early ages of the order. In an historical sketch of the order by Father Leon in Translations of the Aureole Seraphique (p.p. 268-70) it is stated that the habit and capuce were of the poorest material. Originally the size of the capuce varied a little and while some had it sewn to the habit, others wore it loose. The rule was silent as to the colour. The habit of St. Francis, preserved at Florence, is of a gray, or ash colour.

. . . .

The earliest dwelling places of the Friars were undoubtedly of the most primitive style, and in accordance with the

precepts of the founder, expressed by him as follows:
"When they have a competent piece of ground, they are to
"go to the Bishop. . . . . Having
"obtained his blessing, they shall go and make a deep
"ditch all around the land on which they propose to build,
"and a good fence instead of a wall as an emblem of their
"poverty. Then they shall build poor cottages of mud and
"wood, and some few cells for the Friars to pray in, and
"labour for the eschewing of idleness. They shall have
"small Churches, and not large ones, either for preaching
"or on any other pretence."—(Pref. to Mon. Fran., vol. I.,
p. 18.)

The merits of the early Franciscans cannot be denied, and there is undoubted testimony of the strict, if not the actual literal acceptance by them of the stern rule of poverty enjoined by St. Francis. The earliest recorded applications to the Founder to relax the rule of poverty were apparently of no moment, but his unswerving fidelity to the rule was shown by his refusal to allow a proprietorship or property in books, which some of the Friars had acquired. The invariable answer of St. Francis seems to have been, "whoever will be a friar minor, must possess "nothing more than his habit, or carry shoes, if necessary." It was only after the Founder's death that the extremely harsh rules were modified, but the trifling relaxations which were allowed eventually caused a breach, which ended in the division of the Order into two sections, one of which ("The Observants") still professed to observe the founder's rules intact, while the other ("The Conventuals") permitted certain modifications.

* * * * * *

The exact date when the peaceful invasion of England by the Franciscan Friars became an accomplished fact is involved in some obscurity. The Annalists of the Order say that it was in A.D. 1220, and various reasons and quotations are given in support. On the other hand, certain eminent men, skilful in estimating the value of M.S. Chronicles bearing on the subject, favour A.D., 1224-5. Much controversial matter is involved in the discussion, but apparently the discrepancies in the dates do not involve anything of importance, and therefore no good object would be served by entering into the details of the controversy. It seems to be undisputed that Brother Agnellus de Pisa, who was appointed by St. Francis to be the first Minister Provincial of the Order in England, and eight companions, were conveyed from France to Dover, at the expense of certain Benedictine Monks, of Fescamp, in Normandy. Father Leon, in his Historical Sketch, vol. IV., p. 307, says, that " the little band of nine Friars proceeded to Canterbury, "where they were hospitably entertained by the Benedictines, "and then taken in at what was styled, the 'Poor Priests' "Hospital.'" The first established Convents of the Order in England were those of Canterbury, London and Oxford. After the establishment of the Oxford Convent, which was a very primitive dwelling place, and which was first inhabited about the year 1224-25 (other dates have also been given), Brother Agnellus proceeded without delay to establish Convents in various parts of England. At a little later period the Friars built large and substantial conventual buildings at Oxford, and this course seems to have been followed in other places, the old buildings having ceased to provide sufficient accommodation for the increase in the number of the inhabitants. Ere three decades had elapsed from the first coming of the Friars, much progress had been made by them in this country. That the Franciscan Order should have produced from the English province the greatest scholars, the greatest logicians and disputants, and the most profound and subtile intellects—including the celebrated Roger Bacon, Duns Scotus, Alexander Hales, Peecham and others—is as strange as it is true. But, although the founder of the order was able, during his life, to check any attempt on the part of the Friars generally to devote themselves to systematic study, it was to be expected that after his death amongst the large number of men brought into the organization from various parts and under different circumstances, there would be found some examples of giants in intellect as well as in stature. This, however, is only one of several reasons which might be adduced in explanation of what is the most interesting fact in the history of the English Minorites.

The Friars Minors,
or
Gray Friars of Bristol.

Chapter I.

THERE are no authentic records in existence from which it is possible to ascertain the precise period when the Friars Minors first established their habitation in Bristol. It is not improbable that, as was the case elsewhere, the Friars on their arrival took possession of a building already in existence, or they may have erected some rude shelter in the suburbs of the town as a temporary home.

Seyer, the Bristol Historian, who was a conscientious writer, has unwittingly introduced an erroneous statement concerning the foundation of the Bristol House. He has referred to a supposed visit of St. Francis to our city, from which successive writers have drawn incorrect conclusions. In vol. 2, p. 7, the historian says, "Some of our Calendars "say that . . . . in 1226 St. Francis, the "founder of the order, came to Bristol, and that he himself "founded the Nunnery of Lacock, in Wiltshire. The "Convent of the Gray Friars was in Lewins Mead . . " . . . . . it might possibly have been founded by "St. Francis himself while he continued in this neighbour-"hood."

The statement as to the visit of the founder of the order to Bristol must be considered one of the numerous local legends of mystical birth, because it so happens that *he was never in England*. Local "Chronicles" are very free and easy in the combination of fact and fiction. In a list of local events, given in chronological order in "The Memorialist," published in 1823, we are informed that, in 1246, St. Francis *died in Bristol*. The demand for material, on easy terms, by writers of what purports to be local historical information, seems to have tempted the imaginative faculty of the purveyors of fiction to supply for local consumption some meagrely covered stories in the guise of "Chronicles." Chatterton was by no means the first, and he was certainly not the last, to furnish from doubtful sources "copy" for Bristol writers.

With regard to the approximate date of the foundation of the Bristol house of the Friars Minors there is some probability, but no certainty, that it was founded by Bro. Agnellus very shortly after he left Oxford to establish houses in many parts of the country. There is reason to believe that Bristol was one of the earliest settlements of the Friars, but it is conjecture only, and we must be content with the more reliable, but rather scanty, information on the subject which is to be found in the State Rolls and the Chronicles relating to the order.

From the following entry, taken from Eccleston's Chronicle, it will be seen that the Friars must have been established in Bristol at least some little time prior to the

date of the death of Bro. Agnellus, "Factum est autem
"post haec ut mitteruntur speciales visitatores in Angliam,
"qui causa visitationis capitula celebrabant. Primus autem
"visitator Angliae fuit Frater Willelmus de Colvile Senior
"qui capitulum suum celebravit Londoniae sub Fratre
"Agnello, ubi Dominus W. Joymer capellum suis sumptibus
"aedificavit, et tunc temporis introitum in eandem cum
"memorabili gloria celebravit. Post haec venit Frater
"Johannes Naverius qui tunc primo portavit expositionem
"Regulae secundum dominum Gregorium nonum : qui Lon-
"doniae, et Leycestriae, et Bristolliae, similiter etiam fratres
"novicios in maxima multitudine sub Fratre Agnello
"visitationis gratia convocavit."—(Mon. Fran. vol. 1, p. 29.)

[Howbeit it came to pass after these things that special visitors were sent into England, who on the occasion of the visitation celebrated Chapters. But the first visitor to England was Bro. Wm. de Colvile, Senior, who celebrated his Chapter at London under Bro. Agnellus, where Sir W. Joymer built a Chapel at his own cost, and then celebrated his entry into the same with the memorable glory of the time. After these things came Bro. John Naverius, who then first carried the exposition of the rule according to Pope Gregory the Ninth, who at London, at Leicester (and) at Bristol in like manner convoked the Brothers Novitiate in a very great multitude under Bro. Agnellus by favour of the visitation.]

Strange to say the date of the death of Brother Agnellus, who was the first Provincial Minister of England, is not free from doubt, but the historians of the Order state that he died on the 13th day of March, $123\frac{2}{3}$, under which date he was placed amongst the Holy Men of the Order in the Franciscan Martyrology. He was succeeded in the office of Provincial Minister by Bro. Albert de Pisa (Coll. Anglo. Mino. p. 35).

That the Friars were in residence in the year 1234, is evidenced by an entry in the Close Rolls, of 19, Hen. III., p. 1., memb. 26, "The Friars Minors of Bristol shall have "seven cartloads of wood for their hearth, out of the Wood "of Furch, the gift of the King." "Furch," or "Furches" was the ancient name of a portion of Kingswood. In the year 1236, the King gave the Friars fifteen Oaks "in the Wood of Furch"—(Claus. 20. Hen. III. memb. 9). It is not improbable that they were at this time engaged in the erection of buildings. At a later period the King gave five Oaks in "Dene Forest" to the Bristol Convent (Claus. 40, Hen. III., m. 6.)

It appears that under Brother Haymo de Feversham, who was made the third Minister Provincial of England in 1239 (Coll. Anglo. Mino., p. 44) an enlargement of the areas of some of the Friars places was made, for he said that "he "would rather that the brothers had increased areas, and "should cultivate them, that they could have pottages at home "than beg them from others." This he said on the occasion of the enlargement of the area of the Gloucester Convent, which before—by the neglect of Friar Agnellus—the brethren, for the great part, had mutilated or diminished, ("mutilaverant") and afterwards with great difficulty, by Sir Thomas de Berkeley, through the wisdom of his devoted wife, had been restored.—(Mon. Fran., vol. I. p.p. 34, 35). This somewhat remarkable statement has been introduced because it correctly represents the policy afterwards pursued by the Friars with regard to the acquisition of land for cultivation. This declaration of policy which contains an important modification of the Founders rule, must be regarded as authoritative, inasmuch as Bro. Haymo was held in such high repute that he was almost immediately after his election, as Minister Provincial of England, summoned to Rome, and subsequently made Minister General of the whole order of Friars Minors, A.D. 1240.

There was considerable activity shewn by the order in England about this time, and towards the year 1250, in the building of convents and the extension of areas, and at some time before the last mentioned year, the habitation of the Bristol Friars was changed, " Sub Fratre Willelmo mutatus " est locus Eboraci, et similiter locus Bristolliæ, necnon et " locus de Bridgewater sed et locus de Grimsby locus et " Exoniæ sufficientur ampliatus."—Mon. Fran. vol. I. p. 35). It is presumed that the change, which may have been from a temporary shelter to a permanent home, took place under Brother William, of Nottingham, who succeeded Brother Haymo, as Minister Provincial of England, in 1240 ; but it can only be safely asserted that it happened before the year 1250, the date of the ending of the Chronicles of Eccleston, in which the entry appears. In another Chronicle (Lelandi Collectanea IV. p. 341) the name of William " de Abyngdon " is mentioned as the Minister Provincial, but no such name can be found in the list of Ministers Provincial, given by the Historians of the order. The last mentioned Chronicle (Lelandi Collectanea) contains an entry which confirms the succession (after Bro. Haymo) of William " of Nottingham." "Frater Haymo per unum annum ministravit " in Anglia, et postea in generalem electus est. Successit " autem Vicarius suus Frater *Gul de Notingham.*"

Dr. Brewer seems to have formed an opinion that it was to the population in the suburbs of large towns that the attention of the Friars was first directed, and he quotes the fact that in London, York, Warwick, Oxford, Bristol, Lynn, and elsewhere, the convents stood in the suburbs (Preface to Mon. Fran. vol. I. p. 17). Dr. Brewer's conjecture, so far as the Bristol Friars were concerned, is, so far as can be ascertained, unsupported by any evidence. It is almost inconceivable that when the Friars first came to Bristol, they pitched their tents extra muros for the benefit of the "Outsiders." The Friars were par excellence, the Missionaries to the Town, and they were guided and directed by men who possessed much worldly wisdom and insight. They probably preferred the suburbs of Bristol because, first, they were aware of, and desirous, if possible, to disarm the jealousy of the secular clergy, intra muros, who, on account of the lives they, or at least a considerable number of them, were leading (see pref. to Mon. Fran. p.p. 16-17) must have had grave misgivings as to the extent of their hold upon the townsmen, whose lately acquired additional liberty made them less amenable to the spiritual power secondly, but by no means an unimportant factor in the calculation of the Friars, there was the question of obtaining sufficient land for cultivation. "Two of the Mendicant "Orders (in Bristol) the Carmelites and Franciscans (White "and Gray Friars) possessed large tracts of land near their "convents, which were cultivated by their own labour and "skill, as they were partly maintained by the sale of their "produce. They taught the art of horticulture, then rarely "known to or practised by others"(Dallaway p.128). Thirdly, there has occurred another reason, somewhat problematical, it must be admitted, for the selection of a site in Lewins Mead. We have evidence before us of the friendship of the Benedictine Monks for the Order of St. Francis. The gift of the little Church of the Portiuncula, near Assisi, by the Benedictine Monks of Monte Subiaco (see Intro., p. vi.); the transportation of the Friars from France to Dover, at the expense of the Benedictines of Fescamp (see Intro., p. ix.): their reception by the Benedictine Monks at Canterbury (see Intro., p. ix.), together with other marks of favour, shewn them by the same order seem to afford an appearance of a continuity of friendship of a sufficient character to justify us in hazarding a conjecture that the Benedictines of St. James's Priory were the earliest friends of the Franciscan Friars upon their first arrival in Bristol. Herein may, perhaps, be found the reason for the absence of any record as to the source from which the friars obtained their lands, gardens, orchards, &c. Diligent searches have been made for any charter, grant, or license relating to the somewhat large tract of land within the Friars Inclosure, but without any result.

Of course these searches are not conclusive, but it is impossible to help thinking, in the absence of proof to the contrary, that the Friars were originally given the land for their house and surroundings by the Prior and Monks of St. James, or by the Abbey of Tewkesbury, to which Abbey the Priory of St. James was a cell, either on their first arrival in Bristol, or at a little later period, when they were fairly well established. The lands of the Priory of St. James were very extensive, and we find that both on the Northern and the Eastern sides, at various points, the lands of the Monks and Friars were separated only by a narrow lane. The Wills of Bristol townsmen prove that certain property in Lewins Mead belonged to the Abbey of Tewkesbury. There is some slight additional evidence of a negative character to be found in the fact that crown licenses, authorizing the Friars to hold small parcels of land, notwithstanding the Statute of Mortmain (see p.p. 51 and 58) were granted to them, but that with regard to the larger portion, and practically to the whole of their Inclosure, so far as can at present be ascertained, no license was asked for or granted. The Benedictine lands were already in mortmain, and no crown license would have been required. The date of the gift or grant of this land to the Friars is all important in determining whether or not a Crown license was a sine qua non. A brief summary of what might be described as an invasion of a Benedictine Abbey by a party of Minorites, under circumstances which apparently justified Matthew Paris (Anno 1235) in making a charge (the first recorded) against the English Minorites, may not be quite irrelevant. "Under cover of darkness," he asserts, "they would erect a wooden altar, place it on "a small consecrated stone slab, brought for the purpose. "and celebrate a mass. Having thus gained an ecclesiastical "footing, they would hear confessions, say masses, and "even despatch messengers to Rome, to obtain substantial "concessions. These would often be yielded by the "monks from fear of a scandal, and from dread of "the power already gained by the Order at the Court "of Rome itself."—(Mon. Fran., vol. II., p. 12). But notwithstanding the probabilities of the case, it is clear that in the absence of any written testimony, it is impossible to get beyond conjecture. Unfortunately, it must, we fear, be accepted as a fact that the written records of the Provincial Convents of Friars Minors perished when those houses were dissolved; but it must not be forgotten that the Friars' records, whatever they may have been, or whatever form they may have taken, would not, in all probability, have extended back for a sufficient length of time to have enabled us to obtain a complete insight into their proceedings in their early years, because it is almost certain that, for some time after their establishment in Bristol, the strict rule of poverty, which debarred them from even the possession of writing materials, was literally observed. We are not, however, left entirely in the dark as to the methods adopted by those having the control of the English Province, with a view to the development and extension of the work of the Order.

One of the chosen methods for assisting the Friars in their labours and studies is related by Eccleston, who tells us that "Readers were appointed at Hereford, Leicester, "Bristol, Cambridge, and Oxford ; and the gift of wisdom "so overflowed in the Province of England that before the "deposition of William of Nottingham there were as many "as thirty lecturers in England, and a regular succession of "them was provided in the Universities." From the same authority we learn that Friar Gilbert de Cranforth was one of the readers assigned to Bristol.

The historians of the order give credit for the first establishment of a few readers to Albert de Pisa, the second Minister Provincial of England.

In testification of the zeal shewn by the Friars in perfecting their organization, Eccleston informs us that within thirty years after their arrival in England their number in this country alone amounted to 1,242, that they counted 49 Convents in different localities, and that, notwithstanding the jealousy with which they were regarded by the clergy and the Monastic Orders, the Friars multiplied rapidly in London, Canterbury, Oxford, Cambridge, Hereford, Lynn, and Norwich on the East, and Bristol and Bridgwater on the West.

Brother Francis Harold, the epitomizer of Bro. Luke Wadding's Annals of the Friars Minors, says that when St. Bonaventure held a General Chapter of the Order at Narbonne, in France, in the year 1258, the English Province of Friars Minors (even in those early days) is there reckoned to have had seven Custodies, viz.: I. London, II. York, III. Cambridge, IV. Bristol, V. Oxford, VI. Newcastle, and VII. Worcester; and Bro. Bartholomus Pisanus,

Anno 1309, enumerates these seven Custodies as then comprising sixty Convents, viz.:

1. London—Custody consisted of these nine Convents, viz.: (1) London, (2) Canterbury, (3) Winchelsea, (4) Southampton, (5) Ware, (6) Lewes, (7) Chichester, (8) Salisbury, and (9) Winchester.

2 York—Custody had seven Convents, viz.: (1) York, (2) Doncaster, (3) Lincoln, (4) Boston, (5) Beverley, (6) Scarborough, and (7) Grimsby.

3. Cambridge—Custody had nine Convents, viz.: (1) Cambridge, (2) Norwich, (3) Colchester, (4) Bury St. Edmund's, (5) Dulwich, (6) Walsingham, (7) Yarmouth, (8) Ipswich, (9) Lynn.

4. BRISTOL—CUSTODY had nine Convents, viz.: (1) Bristol, (2) Gloucester, (3) Bridgwater, (4) Hereford, (5) Exeter, (6) Carmarthen, (7) Dorchester, (8) Cardiff, and (9) Bodmin.

5 Oxford—Custody had eight Convents, viz.: (1) Oxford, (2) Reading, (3) Bedford, (4) Stamford, (5) Nottingham, (6) Northampton, (7) Leicester, and (8) Grantham.

6. Newcastle—Custody had nine Convents, viz.: (1) Newcastle, (2) Dundee, (3) Dumfries, (4) Haddington, (5) Carlisle, (6) Hartlepool, (7) Berwick, (8) Roxborough, and (9) Richmond.

7. Worcester—Custody had nine Convents, viz.: (1) Worcester, (2) Preston, (3) Bridgnorth, (4) Shrewsbury, (5) Coventry, (6) Chester, (7) Lichfield, (8) Lancaster, and (9) Stafford.

To these sixty Convents were subsequently added many others, some of them in England and some in Ireland (Collectanea Anglo-Minoritica).

The head of a Convent was generally designated as the Warden, but he was sometimes called the Guardian.

Each of the Convents had a seal belonging to the office of Warden or Guardian. In cases where the Convent was a Custody of the Order the Warden was the Custos. The seals were distinguished by the description on the rim, one being the seal of such a Custody and the other of such a Convent. The seal of the Bristol Convent contained a representation of St. Anthony of Padua (Collectanea Anglo-Minoritica). No authority can be found for the description of the Bristol Seal, which does not appear to be in the collection at the British Museum.

The following references to the Bristol Convent and Church appear in Stevens' History of Abbeys, Monasteries, &c.:

"Bristol Monastery of Franciscans, Grey-Friars, or "Friars-Minors in Gloucestershire.

"This house is almost buried in oblivion, there being no "other account of it come to my knowledge but the "following dimensions in Mr. Willis's Hist. of Abbeys, "vol. II., p. 326.:

"The Church and Convent of the Friars of St. Francis, "at Bristol, in Lewensmede Street, in the Parish of "St. James, viz.:

"The Choir of the Church contains in length 28 rods or "50 paces.

"The breadth of the Choir contains 9 rods or 18 paces.

"The length of the Nave of the said Church, with the "two great wings, contains 28 rods or 50 paces.

"The breadth of the said Nave, with the two wings, 'contains 27 rods or 52 paces.

"The breadth of the Belfry Square Tower contains 4 rods or 7 paces.

"There are four Arches in the North Aisle of the Church "and as many in the South."

This is literally translated from the Latin, and after it follow these words:

"Minors. The length of the Church of the Friars-Minors, at Bristol, contains 54 steppys; the breadth contains 52 steppys."

"Now the *Franciscans* and the *Minors* being the same, as has often been repeated, these two accounts are of the same Church; and we find that the breadth is the same, being in both 52 paces, however the difference is in the length, which plainly appears to be a mistake in the latter, there being no likelihood that the Church should be so near square as to be only two paces longer than it was broad" (Stevens, vol. I., p. 158).

In consequence of the discrepancies in the references, it is desirable to give an explanation. According to the measurements of William of Worcester, given at p. 184 of his Itinerarium, it appears that the length of the Nave was "64 gressibus," or 128 feet, and the Choir "54 gressibus," or 108 feet; total length, 236 feet.

The Franciscan Church is mentioned in connection with certain procedings taken by the Bishop of Worcester, in the year 1279, against certain persons, for infringing the right of sanctuary (one of the privileges of the Church) by apprehending one William de Lay, who had taken refuge in the churchyard of St. Philip and Jacob. A part of the punishment of the offenders was "to go from the Church of the Friars Minors, in Lewins Mead, to the Church of St. Philip and Jacob, through the streets naked except their breeches and shirts for four market days for four weeks, each receiving discipline all the way" (Evans, p. 66).

In the year 1334 there were ordained in this Church by the Bishop of Worcester 73 Priests, 39 **Deacons**, 150 Sub-Deacons, and 171 Acolites (Barrett, p. 400).

The Convent was an important one, and belonging to it were extensive gardens, orchards, and fishponds.

Various writers of Bristol History have stated that the Church and Convent of the Grayfriars formerly occupied the site of the present Lewins Mead Chapel, but it is beyond doubt that a blunder has been made. The Lewins Mead Chapel site, the curtilage, and surroundings were originally part and parcel of the lands belonging to the Hospital of St. Bartholomew, which stood contiguous thereto. The rental of St. Bartholomew lands, which now forms part of the endowment of the Bristol Grammar School, includes the ground rent of £5, which was reserved when the lease of the Chapel site was granted. Researches at the Council House, and at the offices of the Bristol Charity Trustees, have afforded positive proof that the land referred to formed no part of the Franciscan property. It must have been erroneously assumed that Johnny Ball Lane (which is also called Bartholomew Lane in old records in the Council House) formed the boundary line between the "Bartholomew" and the Franciscan lands. Barrett was the first to print this misleading statement, which has been copied without investigation by successive writers. So far as it is possible to speak with precision, it may be said that there is no alternative but to place the Friars Church and Conventual Buildings together with the Cemetery within the lines of two lanes or ways in Lewins Mead, running parallel with each other, and now designated "Blackfriars" and "Whitefriars" respectively, both names of course being misnomers. For a long period after the dissolution, the district was described as "Grayfriars," subsequently it became "the Friars," and some ingenious individual must have invented the above names, possibly through ignorance, but certainly with an utter disregard of the history of the locality. As a consequence many people have been led to believe that the Dominicans (Blackfriars), and the Carmelites (Whitefriars), in former times occupied or owned land in Lewins Mead, which is contrary to the fact. This popular delusion has, without doubt, materially assisted to keep the Grayfriars and their convent in obscurity. With regard to the position of the Cemetery, the first account of Jeremy Green, to whom the property of the Friars was leased after the dissolution (see copy account p.   ) contains the following reference to the Cemetery. "For farm of Cemetery on the West side of "the Church of the said house abutting on a street called "Lewens Mede." It has been ascertained that, about fifteen or sixteen years ago, in making some excavations at the rear of an extensive warehouse in Lewins Mead, at that time in the occupation of Messrs. Gardner, Thomas & Co., (but which was formerly in the occupation of Messrs. Ford & Canning) the workmen employed found in the northeast part a large quantity of human bones. These were from time to time dug up and sold, but the sale was eventually stopped in consequence of the marine store dealers having "declined to buy any more human bones." It appears, also, that when this warehouse was rebuilt, in the year 1851, some human bones were found in several places, and a few years afterwards, in carrying a drain through the warehouse to the main sewer in Lewins Mead, a further discovery was made of bones, and the remains of oak coffins. (The positions where these discoveries were made have been pointed out by persons who were present). There can be no doubt that this extensive warehouse includes within its walls the site of the Cemetery. Had the records of the Convent been in existence, we should probably have found the names of great and rich people who were here buried. It is recorded that Eleanor Percy, daughter of Henry, Earl of Northumberland, and widow of Edward Stafford, Duke of Buckingham, who was beheaded by Hen. VIII., by her Will, date 24th June, 1518, bequeathed her heart to be buried in the Church of the Grayfriars, at London, and her body in the Grayfriars at Bristol.—(Nichols Col. Top. vol. 5, p. 276). In Pryce's History of Bristol (p. 53), it is stated that in the year 1851, there was found in this warehouse "a part of the upper portion of a "beautiful square-headed Perpendicular English window, "which shews that some of the buildings which stood here "must have been erected after the year 1400." The extract from the account of Jeremy Green, enables us to place the Church with some likelihood of accuracy to the East of this warehouse, and in all probability a portion stood at the North-Eastern corner, at which point there is a piece of land which forms part of the Warehouse, but which extends beyond the main West wall thereof. At the time the ground was disturbed about 15 or 16 years ago, a considerable quantity of bones were dug up at this point, and during the progress of the alterations a piscina was discovered.

It has been ascertained by actual perusal of deeds relating to portions of property now forming part of the warehouse of Messrs. Champion & Co., in Lewins Mead, that the Friars Orchard was located in this part of the Mead, and extended some distance back in a Northerly direction, and that the land, beyond, and extending to Upper Maudlin Street (formerly Maudlin lane), was originally the gardens of the Convent. There is a tradition, which is confirmed by living witnesses, that an Eastern wall of a portion of the conventual buildings had loopholes and embattlements. This wall, or some part of it, has been incorporated with, and forms part of certain houses on the West side of the way or lane, known as "Whitefriars," and it is in close proximity to a place called "Friar's Court." The prison of the convent may have been located in the building of which the embattled wall originally formed part. That the convent was a strong place is borne out by one of the records of the Berkeley family, quoted by Dugdale. It appears that James Lord Berkeley, nephew of Thomas, 12th Lord Berkeley, who died in 1416, claimed by right Berkeley Castle, but he was opposed in his claim by Margaret, eldest daughter of the Earl of Warwick, and wife of John Talbot, Earl of Shrewsbury. She having corrupted Rice Tewe, the porter of the Castle, procured ingress for her son, Lord Lisle, with a number of armed men, who seized Lord James and his four sons and kept them in prison eleven weeks, and eventually carried them with strong guards into the Grayfriars at Bristol—(Dugdale Baron. 1363). In Smyth's "Lives of the Berkeleys," it is stated that they were "brought to the Gray fryars at Bristoll with great multitude of people warlike arrayed." By virtue of one of the rules of the order, it was necessary, in order to deal with refractory members, that prisons should be constructed, but the incident given by Dugdale goes to shew that the prison of the Bristol Convent was at times put to a use other than that for which it was originally intended. The fortifying or strengthening of places in the country or the suburbs of a town calls to mind the insecurity of life and property during the reigns of Henry III and several succeeding Kings, in consequence of the frequency of predatory attacks by midnight marauders. Might was right in country districts At Oxford the Grayfriars had built their convent just outside the city wall, and King Hen. III, by Letters Patent, authorized them to enclose certain land, situate between the convent and the city, "so that a wall with battlements, like "the rest of the wall of Oxford, be drawn about the "habitation aforesaid." The best evidence of the state of the country in the reign of Edward I. is to be found in the recitals and enactments of the Statute of Winchester (13 Edw. I). In consequence of "murders, maimings, robberies, and thefts," the gates of a walled town were to be shut at 9 p.m., and watched until sunrise. No one, unless his host would be responsible for him, was allowed to remain in the suburbs at night. Highways to market towns were to be widened "so that there be neither dyke, tree, nor bush, "whereby a man may lurk to do hurt within two hundred "feet of the one side, and two hundred feet of the other side," and all persons were compelled to have weapons in their houses "according to the quantity of their lands and goods, "for maintenance of the peace according to the Statute." Another Act of the same reign, contains further provisions on the subject, and it declares that "robberies, burnings, "and manslaughter" were committed, and the peace little observed. In an Act of 5, Edw. III, the midnight marauders were referred to as "Roberdesmen, Wastors, and Draw "Latches." There are records in existence which prove that some of the lawless bands committed some rather daring exploits.

The outer boundaries of the Friars Inclosure were stone walls (see p.p. 95 and 96). The northern wall followed something approaching to the present line of the street known as Upper Maudlin Street, although a considerable strip of the land originally within the inclosure now forms part of the street. The street was originally called Maudlin Lane, the name being a corruption of "Magdalen," and was so named from its proximity to the Nunnery of St. Mary Magdalen, which stood on or adjacent to the site of that well-known hostelry, "The King David," now (December, 1892,) in course of re-erection. The street or lane was probably one of the original Church paths to the Priory of St. James. The wall on the eastern side fronted a portion of the lane or street now known as Lower Maudlin Street, but which was formerly known as Lower Maudlin Lane, and in former times probably formed part of the "Priors' Lane" (see p. 29). Here again it must be remembered that large slices of the original inclosure have from time to time been added to the street, which makes it difficult to accurately trace the original line. During the recent demolition of a house at the eastern corner of Lewins Mead and Lower Maudlin Street an opportunity was afforded for examining an ancient archway (the only old portion of the building, and which apparently was incorporated with and used as a foundation for the modern house), which, judging from appearances, may have originally formed the eastern entrance, or one of the entrances, to the Franciscan Inclosure. The archway was quite wide and high enough to admit of the passage beneath it of a cart or wagon. From the eastern or Lewins Mead angle there is very little difficulty in tracing the southern line of the Friars wall with some degree of accuracy, because it is certain that it abutted on Lewins Mead, and there are plans in existence which give approximately the ancient lines of this side of the Mead.

The conjectural plan annexed is founded on a portion of Mr. Godwin's plan, from which has been eliminated the land which clearly never belonged to the Friars. The plan now correctly represents (as near as may be) the extent of the Friars walled Inclosure as it existed at the date of the dissolution of the Convent and in the days of William Wycestre, from whose Itinerarium the following references have been transcribed:

"Via in Parochia Sancti Jacobi in occidentali parte ecclesiæ Sancti Jacobi prope portam principalem introitus ad prioratem Sancti Jacobi et partem muri orientalem fratrum Sancti Francisci" (William Wycestre, Nasmith's Edition, p. 212).

[A street in the Parish of St. James on the west side of the Church of St. James, near the principal gate of entry to the Priory of St. James, and on the east side of the wall of the Friars of St. Francis.]

"Venella magna vocat le pryour ys lane Sancti Jacobi quæ apud le style in angulo cornerii de Lewynsmede usque ad murum extremum directum super Montague Hill, eundo per murum fratrum Sancti Francisci ex una parte et murum monacorum ex orientali, continet usque returnum ad montem Sancti Michaelis directa linea 360 gressus, scilicet sic retornando venellam ad ecclesiam Sancti Michaelis per continuacionem dictæ venellæ versus occidentem" (William Wycestre, Nasmith's Edition, p. 189).

[Great lane called the lane of the Prior of St. James, which, at the stile in the angle of the corner of Lewinsmead up to the outermost straight wall upon Montague Hill, in going by the wall of the friars of St. Francis on the one side and the walls of the monks on the east, contains, as far as the return to the hill of St. Michael in a straight line, 360 paces; that is to say, in so returning the lane to the Church of St. Michael by continuation of the said lane towards the west.]

[NOTE.—The description, "Montague Hill," in 1480, was probably applied to the whole of the hilly ground extending to Kingsdown. It certainly did not represent the road or hill now known by that name. It is believed that the "Prior's Lane" commenced at the eastern end of Lewins

Mead, and included a portion of the lane now called "Alfred Hill."]

"Venella a capite anguli muri fratrum minorum vocat "le pryour lane monachorum in parte occidentali sic eundo "ad montem Sancti Michaelis versus ejus ecclesiam usque "ad locum et montem vocat Styp Strete prope fontem de "frestone, continet — gressus" (William Wycestre, Nasmith's Edition, p. 189).

[Lane from the head corner of the wall of the Friars Minors called the lane of the Prior of the Monks on the west side, so in going to the hill of St. Michael towards his (sic) Church up to the place called "Styp Strete," near the well of "frestone," contains   paces.]

"Via longa, sive venella, de fine viæ Lewenysmede "ex opposito cimiterii Sancti Jacobi, eundo per hostium "prioris religionum dictæ ecclesiæ, et sic continuando ad "extremam partem dictæ viæ venellæ per muros gardinorum "fratrum Sancti Francisci ad quendam montem acutum in "boriali parte dictæ viæ extrema, et retornando per aliud re- "tornum viæ ducentis versus montem ecclesiæ Sancti Michaelis "continet dicta via sive venella erecta 300 gressus. Et "retornum dictæ viæ ad partem orientalem per murum "dictorum fratrum minorum usque ad venellam eundo ad "ecclesiam Sancti Michaelis, et sic continuando directe "orientaliter usque ad altam crucem petræ erectæ de "frestone cum fonte clausa de frestone ad altiorem, finem "viæ veniente de Ecclesia Sancti Bartholomei vocatum "Stype Street, continet 600 gressus" (William Wycestre, Nasmith's Edition, p. 212).

[Long Street or Lane, from the end of Lewinsmead Street, opposite the churchyard of St. James, in going by the small door or gate of the Prior of the religious of the said church, and in so continuing to the far side of the said street or lane *by the walls of the gardens of the Friars of St. Francis* to a certain sharp hill on the extreme north part of the said street, and in returning by another return of the street leading towards the hill of the Church of St. Michael, contains in the said street or lane made straight 300 paces. And the return of the said street to the east side by the wall of the said Friars Minors up to a lane in going to the Church of St. Michael, and in so continuing directly eastward up to the high cross of stone, built of "frestone," with a well enclosed with "frestone," to the higher end of the street coming from the Church of St. Bartholomew, called "Stype Street," contains 600 paces.]

These references and measurements are given for what they are worth; they are certainly of some value, and afford information on certain points which, but for the industry of William Wycestre, would have been lost for ever.

.   .   .   .

A careful examination of the district situated between the present northern line of the street called Lewins Mead and an imaginary line drawn through Upper Maudlin Street will give some slight idea of the advantages which the Friars enjoyed by reason of the situation of their inclosure. They possessed a broad tract of land, well sheltered from the north, containing naturally formed plateaus and gentle slopes, lying open to the south, which were particularly favourable for early and profitable culture. The soil of a portion of the land abutting on Lewins Mead was alluvial, and the Friars had under their dominion a bounteous supply of water, which, by reason of its rise in the higher land, could be carried at their will to any part of their inclosure, and the river below afforded every facility for drainage. These natural advantages were of no small importance to men who derived a substantial portion of their sustenance from the cultivation by their own hands of land which was held in common for their benefit, and it does not entail any great stretch of the imagination to picture a little community of contented bachelors! living in the suburbs in a snug sheltered position, among pleasant surroundings, and in the possession of almost everything that would be likely to conduce to sound bodily health and tranquility of mind.

. . . .

The remains of the work and buildings of the Friars which still exist may be briefly described as follows:

1. The conduit head and reservoir, situate under certain land and houses on the north side of Upper Maudlin Street,(*) with the leaden pipes and arched subways. The leaden main pipe remains in its original position under a portion of the land formerly the gardens of the Friars, but which now forms the burial ground attached to the Moravian Chapel, and is continued under a portion of the premises occupied in connection with the Board School. At this point (†) it is carried underneath the steps leading from the Board School to Lewins Mead, thence the water is conveyed, *via* Lewins Mead (the line of which is followed as far as the Lewins Mead Chapel, and outside the courtyard of this building there is a stop-cock) St. John's Bridge, Christmas Street, Broad Street, and Corn Street to the tap in All Saints' Lane, adjoining the Church. Mr. William Scott Lawrence, who formerly carried on an extensive business as a plumber, states that

---

(*) The main reservoir is constructed about 93 feet from the pavement on the north side of the street, and there are three filter beds between it and the street. There is a branch subway, about 330 feet in length, with a reservoir and two filter beds. The main supply passes through beds of ironstone under the gardens of houses in Bedford Place.

(†) It is probable that the All Saints' branch pipe was here connected to the main, and the branch conduit constructed at the expense of the parishioners.

the subterranean archway and the arrangements for the collection and storage of the water, together with the outfall for the overflow, are of an excellent character, and are splendid examples of the work of the Friars; and he also speaks with enthusiasm of the solidity of the work in connection with the Carmelite's (now St. John's) conduit. Mr. Lawrence, who is now over 80 years of age and quite hale and hearty, has known these two conduits ever since his boyhood, and his earliest recollections, as an apprentice, includes a journey through the subterranean passage of the Carmelite's conduit, which is constructed under Park Street.

2. A building situate at the foot of the steps leading from the Board School to Lewins Mead (on the left or eastern side going from the school to Lewins Mead), the walls of which are in a fair state of preservation. This building, which runs north and south, has been structurally altered by the addition of floors, partitions, windows, &c., and is now divided into two dwelling houses under one roof. Mr. T. S. Pope's measurements are 31 feet 6 inches by 11 feet 6 inches in the clear, and the heighth, from ground floor to apex of roof in the clear, is about 29 feet. There appears to have been an outer hall or lobby at the back of the building, from which apparently access from the ground floor to the land on the higher level was gained by means of a flight of steps. Portions of the wall of this outer hall still exist, and on the higher level there are the remains of an original wall and buttress. There seems to be very little doubt that the old building was divided by a floor into two apartments. The upper one, which probably constituted the hall of the Friars, was reached by stairs built between the two existing walls,* and it was lighted from the west by two pointed Gothic windows

* The stairs were lighted from the east by a small window. See sketch No. 14.

of similar design. These windows have been recently revealed as a consequence of a careful examination of the old building. Mr. Pope (who has kindly made a sketch of one of them) considers them to be of the late fourteenth century date, and the mouldings (see sketch, No. 6) shew them to be of good type. The tracery is about 6 inches thick with moulded rear arches, which are particularly good. The roof, a portion of which has been shut out from sight by the addition of a modern ceiling, is pointed or wagon-headed. The oak cornice and ribs are in an excellent state of preservation, and the mouldings (see sketches, Nos. 1 and 2) are very interesting as specimens of early work not often met with. There are the remains of an original stone chimney on the inner side of the west wall (see sketch, No. 8). There is a curious little air inlet on the western side, which gives a character to the roof. In the wall of the lower apartment, facing east, there are the remains of a window (see sketch, No. 10). It cannot be stated with certainty to what use the lower apartment was applied, and it must be left open for persons visiting the place to form their own opinion. The main walls of the building average about two feet in thickness.

Having regard to the discovery of the remains of " a beautiful square-headed Perpendicular English window" (ante p. 25) in an adjoining warehouse, we may reasonably conclude that the Friars must have reconstructed some of their buildings towards the end of the 14th century or the early part of the 15th. The old building partly stands on a large vault or cellar (which runs east and west), the present entrance to which is not the original one. During the progress of the alterations in the large warehouse (ante. p. 24) an underground passage was discovered, which converged towards the cellar, but no attempt was made to trace its course beyond the north wall of the warehouse, which stands within a few yards of the present entrance to the cellar. Some stone steps were also discovered which seemed to indicate that the Friars had an entrance to the cemetery from the upper level.

Mr. Robert Hall Warren, who has for a long period taken an active interest in archæological matters relating to the City, states that, about 35 years ago, the late Mr. E. W. Godwin, F.S.A., a well-known and enthusiastic antiquary, informed him that he had "discovered the roof of the "Dormitory of the Gray Friars," of whose conventual buildings it had been thought not a vestige remained. The two gentlemen subsequently visited Lewins Mead and made an inspection of the building which Mr. Warren thinks was "a house directly on the street (Lewins Mead), "but he is in doubt whether the roof ran east and west or "north and south." Mr. Godwin's measurements of the apartment have been preserved. The size was 31 feet by 11 feet 6 inches, which is practically the result of Mr. Pope's measurements of the building at the foot of the steps,

The late Mr. Godwin made some sketches of the roof referred to, and, from tracings supplied by Mr. Warren (see sketches, Nos. 12, 12ª & 12ᵇ), it will be observed that the sections represent work of a different period to that of the roof of the building below the steps, of which sketches have been kindly supplied by Mr. Pope. It is quite possible, therefore, that Mr. Godwin's sketches were taken from a building in Lewins Mead which has since been demolished, and that the remarkable similarity in the measurements is only a coincidence. It should be remembered that it was quite usual to adopt the same moulding in different buildings, and to reproduce new work from sketches of earlier buildings. Mr. John Reynolds (a well-known authority on Archæology) states that many years since he visited the building discovered by Mr. Godwin, and he (Mr. R.) has a strong recollection that it was a house on the northern side of Lewins Mead, and that the entrance to it was directly on the street.

3. There is a passage which commences underneath a house belonging to the Moravian Trustees, which house almost adjoins the last described building. On opening the kitchen floor it was found that there was a long covered way under the ground floor. The sides are constructed of large stones put together without mortar or cement, but the arch (which is of considerable extent) is very strongly formed of thick stone and cement. In the south wall of the house (underneath the kitchen) there is an arch (see sketch, No. 11) which has been partly filled in with debris, but it is about 5 feet in heighth. It is possible that this passage, which is carried under other houses in the direction of the river, was used to carry off the overflow of a portion of the water supply of the Convent. The underground passage and arch were probably constructed in the 14th century. The house is, however, of much later date, and is of the Jacobian style of architecture.

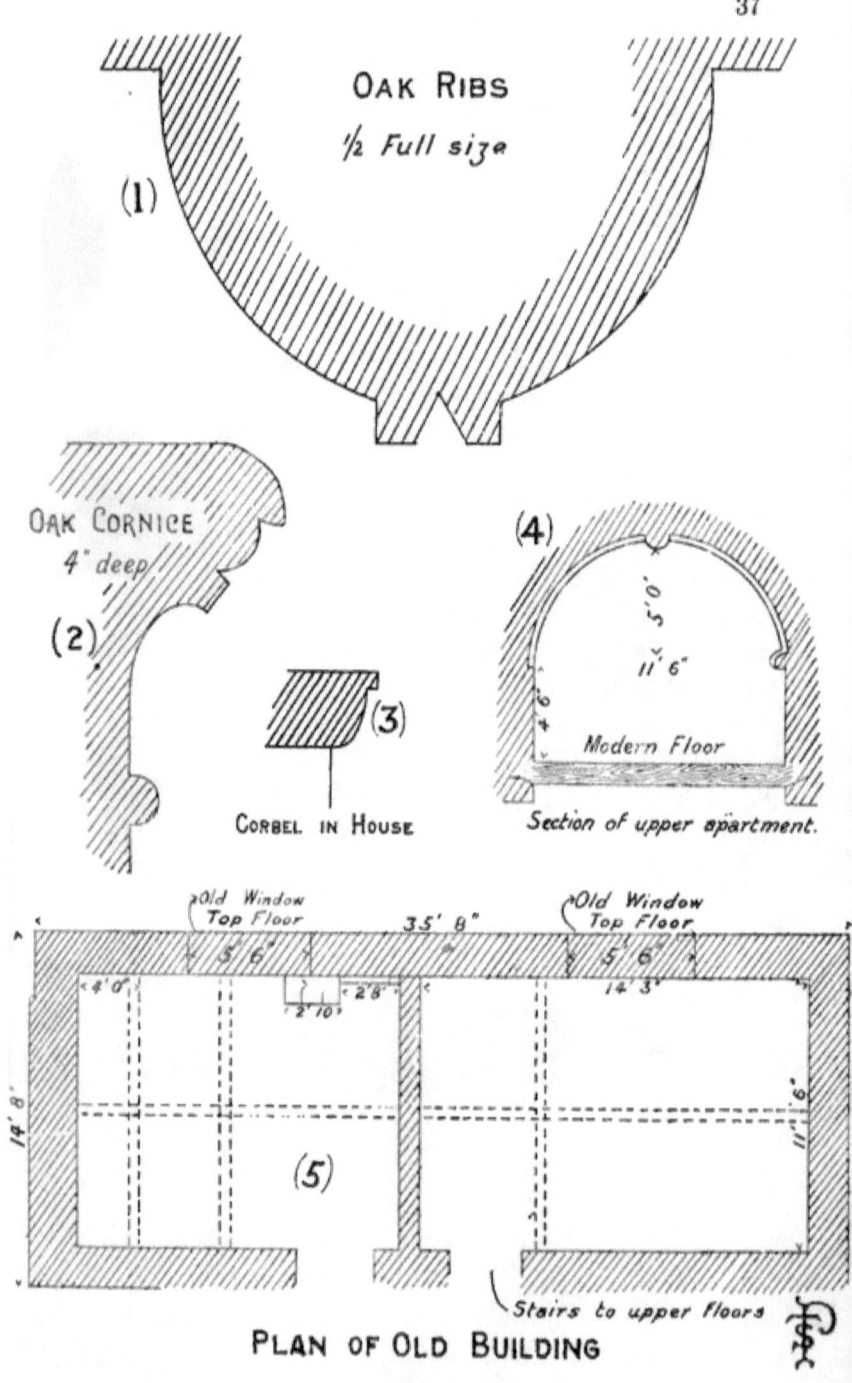

39

(6) OLD WINDOW. Top Floor.

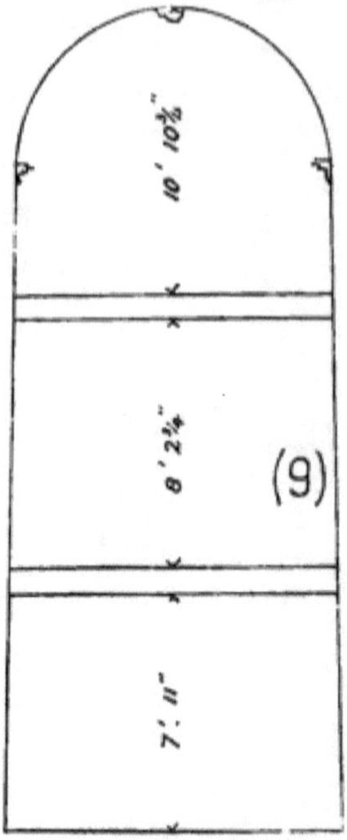

(7) Jamb of Old Window.

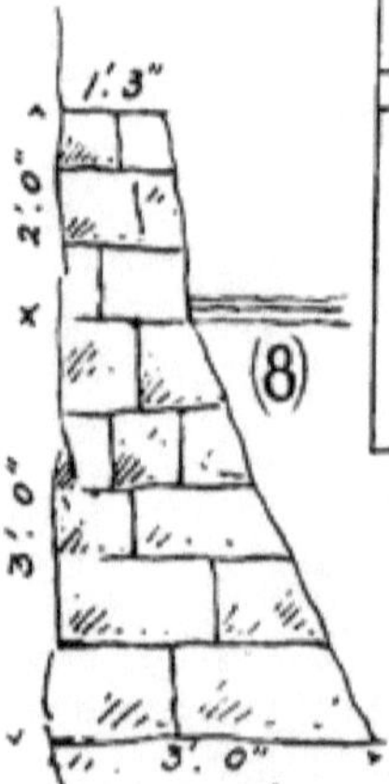

(8) Old Stone Chimney.

(9) SECTION OF OLD BUILDING.

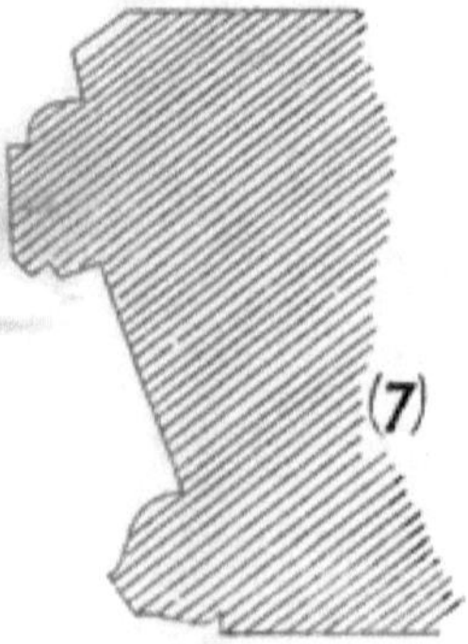

(10) HEAD OF WINDOW IN SCULLERY

41

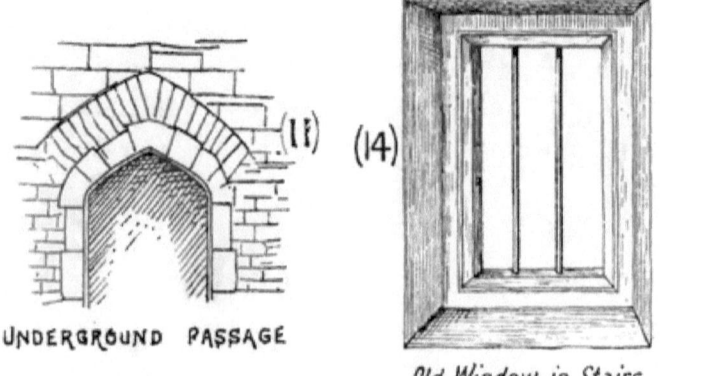

UNDERGROUND PASSAGE

Old Window in Stairs.

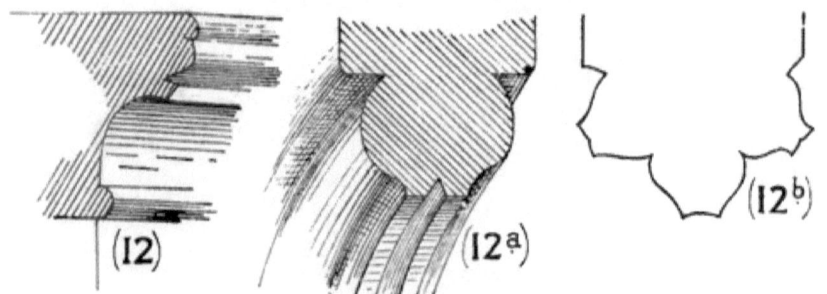

DETAILS of ROOF (open Timber)
Franciscan Friars, BRISTOL.

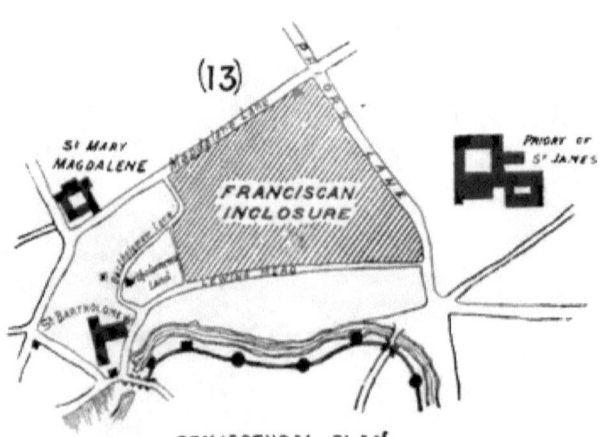

CONJECTURAL PLAN.
*John & Ball Lane otherwise Johnny Ball Lane.

Chapter II.

THE difficulties to be encountered by the would-be historian of the houses of all or any of the Mendicant Friars in Bristol, or elsewhere, are well-known to antiquaries, and to those who have made a study of the subject. In the particular case of the Friars Minors, it is believed that, with the exception of the London Convent, no record of the English houses exists, hence the difficulty in obtaining accurate and trustworthy information of the history of the provincial Convents and Churches.

The destruction of the various documents relating to the Conventual houses, together with the MS. books, which represented the almost invaluable literary labours of the Friars, is much to be deplored, and is regarded by many persons, whose opinions are entitled to consideration, to have been one of the most unjustifiable acts of those to whom the work connected with the suppression of the religious establishments was entrusted. Any attempt, therefore, to deal with the history of a provincial Convent of Friars Minors necessitates searches amongst the State rolls and records, which must be regarded for all practical purposes as the principal sources from which information can be obtained. Items of information relating to a particular Convent are to be found in unexpected places, but the searches connected therewith involve a considerable sacrifice of time. The

Chronicles of the thirteenth century occasionally throw a little light on the subject, but having regard to the scanty materials in existence, much information of a reliable character cannot be expected.

One of the earliest public acts to which the Friars Minors devoted themselves was the "preaching" and promoting the crusades, and one of these was preached by them in the year 1234, in conjunction with the Friars Preachers (the Dominicans or Black Friars). The Rev. C. F. R. Palmer (of St. Dominics Priory, London), who is the greatest living authority on the history of the Friars Preachers of England, having been appealed to for information, has sent the following reply: " It is certain that, in conjunction " with the Friars Preachers, the Friars Minors were active " in proclaiming the matter of the Holy Land throughout " the length and breadth of the kingdom." In connection with the preaching of the Crusade in 1250-1 certain letters patent were committed to the care of Prior de Aldesworth, of the Bristol Friars Preachers, in which the King made a distinct promise in order to remove a misapprehension which had arisen as to the liability of persons assuming the Cross (Pat. Roll. 35, Henry III., m. 13). Several reliable Chronicles of the Thirteenth Century couple the two orders of Friars on various occasions when it was ordered that a Crusade should be preached (Matthew Paris. Chronica Majora, vol. IV., p. 287. Annales de Theoksberia, A.D. 1252. Wyke Chronican, A.D. 1268).

In the absence of the records of the Bristol House we are left without a list of the Wardens, but occasionally the name of one of these office holders is found in some out-of-the-way place. We are enabled to give the name of a Warden who held office in Bristol in the latter part of the thirteenth century, together with a little information as to his family, from an old Register at present in the Bishop's Registry at Hereford.

It appears by the Register of Richard de Swynfield, who was Bishop of Hereford between A.D., 1282 and A.D. 1316, that Thomas de Swynfield was Warden of the Bristol Convent of Friars Minors (Reg. Swn. f. 62 B). Members of the Swynfield (otherwise Swinfield or Swenfield) family were patrons of the Franciscans, and one of them held an office which, generally speaking, was conferred on the most distinguished men of the order. In the list of "Ministri Provinciales Angliæ" (M.S. Cottonian Nero, A, ix., f. 102) appears the following entry, "Septimus Minister. Petrus de Swenfield, jacet Leycestriæ." Richard de Swynfield was, prior to his appointment to the see of Hereford, in high favour with Thomas de Cantilupe, the then occupant of the Bishopric, whom he succeeded. Bishop Cantilupe, died at Civita Vecchia, on the 25th of August, 1282, in the presence of Richard de Swynfield, who had been at Rome with the Bishop, and with whom he was on his way back to England. Shortly after his return to England, Richard de Swynfield was appointed to the vacant see, which he held for thirty-three or thirty-four years. Bishop Swynfield was a patron of the Franciscans, and the records preserved at the Hereford Diocesan Registry prove that he was a donor of small gifts to several convents of the order, and that he had evinced much interest in the Hereford Convent, which was comprised in the Bristol Custody, of which Thomas de Swynfield was the Warden and Custos. The Franciscans at this period, could justly boast that their order contained the names of some of the most learned men of the day. The Rev. John Webb in his work on the Swynfield "Roll of household expenses," gives a true description of the then state of the Franciscan order, and it is advisable to quote his own words:—

"Pope Nicholas III. who died in 1280, made more Bishops "from among them (the Franciscans) than from any other "order, and they could boast of many persons of eminence "in character, ability, and station. At the time immediately "under consideration, the reigning Pontiff, Nicholas IV, the "late and the present Archbishop, with other Churchmen of "rank were Minorites. There is some probability, though "the evidence on which it rests is rather inferential than "direct, that Swynfield (the Bishop) himself may have been "of that order, for it is plain that he shewed them tokens of "marked attention."—(Abstract and Illustrations of Roll, p.p. 62-3).

The Rev. T. P. Wadley, in his valuable book on "Bristol Wills," quotes a curious entry found by him in the Worcester Diocesan Records: "1308, 12th Kal. Jan. Brother Thomas "de Canyngges, of the Order of Friars Minors, was ordained "priest by the Bishop of Worcester, in the Parish Church "of 'Foleham' Diocese of London."

[NOTE.—The jurisdiction of the Bishop of Worcester was at this period very extensive, and included Bristol].

The name of Thomas de Canynge appears in a list of "Fratrum Minorum Magistri Cantabrigiæ" as follows: "Quadragesimus Octavus frater Thomas de Canynge."

[NOTE.—A century and a half later we shall find that William Canynge was a benefactor of the Friars Minors of Bristol both by Deed (see p. 61) and by Will (see p. 63).

The only other item of local interest in the list of "Fratrum Minorum Magistri Cantabrigiæ" is the following, viz.:— "Sexagesimus Secundus frater Willielmus Dormyntone de "Custodia Bristolliæ."—(Cott. MS. Nero, A. ix., f. 78).

The Chronicles of the order contain the names of several Friars of the Bristol custody, who were selected to hold the important office of Minister Provincial. Under the heading "Ministri Provinciales Angliæ" the following names occur, viz.:

"Vicesimus Minister, frater Johannes de Went, Doctor "theologiæ Oxoniæ de custodia Bristolle, et jacet Herefordiæ."

"Tricesimus quartus Minister, frater Johannes David, " Doctor theologiæ et de custodia Bristolle."

"Tricesimus septimus Ministre, Frater Thomas Radnor, "sacræ theologiæ doctor, de custodiæ Bristolle, et de conventu " Herefordiæ."—(M.S. Nero, A ix., f. 102).

In the list of learned Franciscans of the reign of Edward III, occurs the name of Thomas Staneshaw, or Stanshawe, of Bristol. Brother Stanshawe was called to Avignon, and became a penitentiary (i.e., one who prescribes the rules and measures of penance). He died at Avignon in the year 1346.—(Collectanea Anglo-Minoritica, anno 1346).

In the year 1485, Brother Thomas Whitefield was custos of the custody of Grayfriars, Bristol.—(Barrett p. 400).

The Convent possessed a valuable and an almost unlimited supply of pure water, which passes under houses and gardens in a northerly direction, from a subterranean passage which extends under Upper Maudlin Street, in which street there are two entrances thereto by means of iron doors, one of which is inserted in the pavement just outside the Moravian Chapel courtyard, and the other in the pavement on the opposite or North side of the street.

There has been discovered in the Record Office a very interesting Petition, written in Norman French, which appears to have been presented by the Friars to King Edward III, as to this conduit. This petition contains a recital that the land, &c., had been given to the Friars in the reign of Edward I, by Joan, the widow of John de Lediard. The John de Lediard referred to was Mayor of Bristol in the year 1277, which circumstance serves as some slight guide to the date of the grant, which must, of course,

have been some time after his year of mayoralty. The
curious mode by which the gift was made to the Friars
calls for observation. They were debarred by the rules of
St. Francis from holding property, but an easy and simple
plan of getting over the difficulty had been discovered in the
very earliest days of the English Province of the order. At
Canterbury, London, Oxford, Cambridge, and other towns,
land, and sometimes money, had been vested in the
Corporation in trust for the Friars. The simplicity of the
transactions very probably diverted attention from the
boldness of the innovation thus made in the then existing
laws relating to real property. The vesting of land in the
Commonalty, in trust for the brethren of a particular convent,
rather points to a realisation on a limited scale of the
socialistic suggestion of which much has been lately heard,
that all land and property should be vested in the State or
Commonalty. The grant by Joan de Lediard to the Bristol
Friars was not made to the Corporation, but another and
equally effective device was found for carrying out her pious
wish to benefit the Friars. The grant was made to the
King (Edward I) to the use of the Friars in perpetual
Almoigne (free alms,) the result of which, notwithstanding
any reservation in the license afterwards granted by King
Edward III, would most probably have been that the Friars
were absolved from the suits and services (if any) usually
made and rendered to the lord of the particular fee, and
which were incidental to the tenure of land under the feudal
system. The chief lord or lords of the fee were in many
cases deprived of their legal rights, in consequence of grants
in Almoigne or Frankalmoigne, and the excuse given by the
Church was, that the masses and religious services performed
by the grantees were far more profitable, and of more last-
ing advantage, than any fines, heriots, escheats, or earthly

services could afford to the lords, who were, to a certain extent, practically compelled to submit to the power of the Church. It is somewhat curious that one of the first inroads on the feudal tenures should have been made by the Church. The Friars continued to hold the land, conduit, and fountain without any apparent interruption until the year 1375 (48 Edward III,) but it appears by the petition at that time presented by the Friars to the King that they were in a state of doubt as to the validity of their title, which may have been occasioned by an omission to secure the confirmation of the grant by the heir of Joan de Lediard. They appear to have made no prior application for the King's license to hold &c., notwithstanding the Statute against grants of land to religious houses. But whatever may have been the reason for the friars' petition, the prayer was acceded to, as will be seen by the license or confirmation of the King, and their title was thus rendered complete. The license or confirmation serves to illustrate the way in which the Friars got rid of the little difficulties presented alike by the rule of the order, and the Statute of Mortmain. Apart, however, from the Statute, the transaction affords an apt illustration of the absurdity of the strict rule of St. Francis, for what possible harm could there have been in the acceptance by the Friars of the particular parcel of land, the possession of which was necessary to secure to them a supply of pure water, one of the essentials to their existence, and also of the greatest importance, as the means of keeping the ponds in which they preserved fish for their use, properly supplied with water.

The conduit, which has been now running for six centuries, is the present source of supply of the All Saints' Conduit, as to which Barrett says, "In 1400 the Grand "Prior and Proctor of the Priory of St. James granted the

"Parishioners a little conduit of water to which the spring "rising in Prior's Orchard (now Bird's Garden) was "conveyed, and thence in leaden pipes underground to a "public cistern in Corn Street for the use of the City." Barrett gives no authority for this statement, nor does he quote any document in verification of his statement. Very frequently the historian quotes from original documents, adding in many cases the words "penes me," but in this instance the words do not appear, and we are afforded no clue as to the source from which the information was obtained. If it were not for the existence of this statement as to the source of the supply to the All Saints' Conduit, there would be little or no hesitation in saying that the water was conveyed, either before or after the dissolution of the Convent, by an extension of the leaden pipes to All Saints' Parish. It is not improbable that it was after the dissolution, and when the conventual property together with the conduit and streams of water belonging thereto had passed into the hands of the Corporation, that a better supply of water than the then existing supply being available for All Saints' parish, it was thought advisable to extend the pipes, and carry thither the water. This is precisely what happened at Stafford, the conduit of the Grey Friars having, after the dissolution, been used for the purpose of conveying the water into the town. Barrett's history, while it certainly contains much valuable and original information, is so full of misleading and incorrect statements that it is difficult for those engaged in original researches connected with the history of the city to know what to accept or what to reject. The words "Grand Prior and Proctor" in Barrett's description of the alleged gift of the Conduit are of very doubtful origin, especially the prefix "Grand." A concise description of the Conduit has been already given (ante p. 32).

(COPY PETITION FROM THE FRIARS MINORS OF BRISTOL TO KING EDWARD III.)

" A ñre ĩsredoute f͞r⁽¹⁾ ūre f͞r le Roi supplient ses pou'es
" orato͞'s ffreres Meno͞'s de Bristuyt q̃ come vne Johane de
" Lydiard q̃ iadis feust la fem̃e Johan de Lydiard de Bristuyt
" iadis dona p sa chartre a touʒ iours a noble Roi Edward
" filʒ a Roy Henr̃ ṽre p̃genito͞r au oeps des ffreres meno͞'s de
" mesme la ville en ppetuele almoigne vne rode de t̃re
" ensemblement oue la fonteyn del ewe viue ⁊ la conduit as
" ditʒ freres en les suburbes de Bristuyt a auoir ⁊ tenir p͞r
" chant̃ chescun an deus messes p͞r lalme du dite Johane ⁊
" les ancest̃s ūre f͞r le Roy les queles freres adonqes
" supposantʒ le dit doun estre seure ⁊ sufficeant entrerent
" mesme la t̃re t teñ p v͞rtue del dit chartre ⁊ issint ils ⁊ lous
" successours ount tenuʒ ⁊ occupeʒ les dites t̃res ⁊ teñʒ
" depuis en cea saunʒ autre licence ou garante p quoi plese
" a ṽre ĩsnoble ⁊ t̃sg͞uciouse f͞rie g͞ũnt as ditʒ freres vne
" chartre de pdon del dit ĩspas et outre qils puissent tenir
" meisme la t̃re t tenʒ a eux ⁊ a lo͞r successours p͞r priere p͞r
" vous ⁊ vos p̃genito͞'s ⁊ p͞r la dite Johane solone lentente du
" dit feffement saunʒ empeschement a touʒ iours en oeu'e
" de charite.
" [Endorsed] Ceste bille fust g͞ũnte p ūre f͞r le Roy."

(COPY OF KING'S LICENSE AS TO THE LAND, CONDUIT, &c.)

Extracted from Patent Roll 48, Edward III., Part 1, memt. 2.

" FOR THE FRIARS MINORS OF BRISTOL.

" The King to all to whom, &c., greeting. Know ye that
" whereas a certain Joan de Lidiard formerly the wife of
" John de Lidiard of Bristol lately by her charter demised

(1) Seigneure.

"and granted to Edward son of King Henry formerly King
"of England our grandfather and to his heirs one rood of land
"with the appurtenances in the suburbs of Bristol together
"with the fountain of fresh water and the conduit to the
"use of the Friars Minors of the town of Bristol in free
"pure and perpetual alms to celebrate yearly two masses
"for the soul of the said Joan and for the souls of her
"husband and ancestors and of our ancestors former Kings
"of England for all secular services and demands for ever
"as in the charter aforesaid more fully is contained: And
"now the said Friars have prayed us that whereas they
"and their predecessors had entered upon the said land
"fountain and conduit aforesaid by virtue of the demise
"and grant aforesaid so made to our said grandfather for
"the said Friars and for their use and had possessed them
"up to the present time hoping that they were sufficiently
"valid and secure for them for the reasons aforesaid that
"we would be willing to pardon their transgressions
"committed in this matter and moreover grant that they
"may have and hold to them and their successors for ever
"the said land fountain and conduit aforesaid with the
"appurtenances in the form aforesaid: We from reverence
"to God and in order that the masses aforesaid may be
"yearly celebrated by the said Friars in their house there
"for the souls aforesaid according to the pious intent of
"the said Joan in the form aforesaid of our special grace
"have pardoned the transgressions done in the premises
"willing and granting for us and our heirs as much as in
"us lies that the said Friars and their successors may
"have and hold the said land fountain and conduit with
"the appurtenances to them and their successors to
"celebrate the said masses for the said souls in the form
"aforesaid for ever without let or impediment of us or

"our heirs or our justices escheators sheriffs or other our
"bailiffs or ministers whatsoever. Notwithstanding the
"statute published for not putting lands and tenements in
"mortmain. Saving nevertheless to the chief lords of that
"fee the services thereof due and accustomed.

"In witness whereof, &c.
"Witness the King at Westminster the 14th day of August."

The Friars were also the possessors of the right to a moiety of the prisage ("medietatem prisarum piscium") of all fish (salt and fresh) brought into Bristol. "Prisage" means a right to take toll in kind instead of in current coin. This franchise was enjoyed by the Friars from the reign of Edward II down to the dissolution of their house in the year 1538. The other moiety of the prisage of fish belonged to the Bristol Friar-Preachers (the Dominicans), and was enjoyed by them until the dissolution. This right to take toll of fish in kind seems to have been appurtenant to the Crown, and the two moieties were granted and confirmed by successive sovereigns to the two orders of Friars in Bristol as a charitable gift or royal alms, but there is very little doubt that the Friars regarded it as a right. The grants to the Franciscans and Dominicans were separately made, but the form was very much the same in each case. Subjoined is a copy of the Grant or Letters Patent of King Henry VIII, dated 6th June, 1510, by which the right to the moiety of the prisage was confirmed to the Friars Minors:

(Extract from Patent Roll 2, Hen. VIII., p. 2, m. 14).

"WARDENS AND FRIARS MINORS OF THE TOWN OF BRISTOL.

"The King to all to whom &c. greeting. Know ye that
"we understanding how the Lord Edward the Second after

"the Conquest and others our progenitors late Kings of
"England for the time being severally and successively by
"their Letters Patent out of their charity and alms granted,
"to wit, each of them in his time to the warden and convent
"of the House of the Order of the Friars Minors of the town
"of Bristol the moiety of the prisages of fish as well
"salt as fresh appertaining to the same for the time
"being, to the same warden and convent and to their
"successors for the aid and sustentation of them the said
"warden and convent: We willing to act graciously
"towards the now warden and friars of the said order of
"our special grace and charity have given and granted and
"by these presents do give and grant for us and our heirs
"as much as in us lies to the said warden and friars for
"their relief and support the moiety of the prisages of all
"and singular the fish as well salt as fresh coming and from
"that time to come to the said town as well by land as by
"water: to have and to take to the said warden and friars
"and their successors by their own hands from time to time
"of the alms of us and of our heirs for ever. And this
"without paying or making fine or fee in any way for the
"premises into the hanaper of our Court of Chancery or
"elsewhere to our use.
"In witness whereof &c. Witness the King at Westminster
"the 6th day of June."

The right of prisage, or right to take as toll, specified quantities from goods and merchandize coming to Bristol reads rather oddly at the present day.

It is clear that the mayor had at one time, as "mayor's "dues," certain claims on the fish coming into the town. In the sheriff's return, in the year 1517 (8th Henry VIII.) the following entry appears:—

"Item the Mayor hath . . . . . .
"certaine fisshe of ev'y bote offfishe which
"by estimacion may yerely be worthe $\}$ xiij^{li.} vi^{s.} viij^{d.}
"besides his sedile," which, with other
items, amounted to -   -   -   -   -

The Mayor was entitled (in addition to certain rights to salt fish) to prisage of fish as follows:—

"Of ev'ie boate of Milwell and Lingg - vj. of them
"   „   „   of fresh camps   -   - ij. of them
"   „   „   of Thorbecks and Tynbies - iiij. of them
"   „   „   of Soles and Places   - xij. of them
"   „   „   of Breames   -   -   - xij. of them
"   „   „   of fresh Hake   -   - vj. of them
"   „   „   of Haddocks   -   - viij. of them
"   „   „   of Shades   -   -   - viij. of them
"   „   „   of Mackrells   -   - viij. of them
"   „   „   of Cockles   -   - a bushell of them
"   „   „   of Muskels   -   - a bushell of them
"   „   „   of Oysters   -   -   - ije. of them

"If any of the said boates that dooth bring Oysters, "Cockells or Muskels doe bring Ffish, then take the Ffish "and leave the Oysters, Cockells and Muskells" (MSS. British Museum).

A few records of other gifts, benefactions, &c., to the Friars still exist, and deserve to be quoted.

One of the earliest charitable gifts is thus recorded, "Mary daughter of Edward I. and Eleanor of Castile came "to Bristol in May 1304 and before leaving the town she "gave 20/- to the Friars Minors and Friars Preachers" (Rot. Gard. Expensiæ duæ Mariæ fil. regis 32, Edw. 1.)

Thomas, Lord Berkeley, the second of that name, who was born at Berkeley, A.D. 1245 (29, King Hen. III.) shortly after his grandfather's death, spent "his next dayes "at Bedminster by Bristoll." . . . . . Having as his guides and instructors, "the Abbot and Prior of St. "Augustines Monastery by Bristoll and the Master of "St. Katherines Hospitall (confyning upon this Manor of "of Bedminster) creatures begot by his ancestors alms and "devotions," by deed of 1st June, 1307, gave (inter alia) to the Bristol Friars yearly during his life-divers quarterns of wheat out of the several granaries of his manor houses. The next Lord Berkeley, Thomas, the third of that name (1326-1361) caused a payment to be made to the Friars Minors of Bristol when they went to the General Chapter of the Order, and this same lord on another occasion (9th year) when the Friars were taxed to pay a certain duty to the King sent them "either all or most part of "the money in case thereof" (Smyth's "Lives of the "Berkeleys").

William Golde by will, dated 25th April, 1329, bequeathed a legacy to the Friars, "Item lego fratribus Minoribus "Bristoll ij. libras seri" (Berkeley Castle Wills). Maurice Chapstowe's Will, bearing date the 2nd July, 1342, contains the following: "Item fratribus Minoribus Bristoll vid." (Berkeley Castle Wills). The will of John Wale, bearing date 18th October, 1348, contains a legacy to the Friars Minors of Bristol (Berkeley Castle Wills).

Ralph de Salop, Bishop of Bath and Wells, by will, dated 12th May, 1363, ordered the residue of his goods to be divided into three parts, the second of which he gave to religious men, including the Friars Minors and the other three Orders of Mendicant Friars of Bristol and other places (Reg. Episc, Bathen et Well).

Robert Gradely (or Grately), by his will, dated 1385, September 26th, desired to be buried in the Church of the Friars Minors of Bristol, where the bodies of his wives were interred. Testator gave legacies to the Mother Church of Worcester, and to that of the Parish Church of St. John of Bristol, and to the Rector of the same Church. To the said Friars he gave a whole cloth of blanket "p'courcell inde facien." To each Order of Mendicant Friars in Bristol five shillings—(Bristol Wills).

In the year 1386 the Friars received, by way of a gift, from five worthy citizens of Bristol (Walter Frampton (or Frompton), Elias Spelly, John Vyel, Thomas Knapp, and Walter Tidestyle) a "toft" (*i.e.*, a piece or parcel of land, upon which a decayed messuage then or formerly stood) with the appurtenances, as an easement to their house. On the 16th October, 1386, King Richard II. gave the necessary license to the Friars to hold the land, notwithstanding the Statute, &c. It is a matter of conjecture as to the position of the "toft," or for what purpose it was secured. The land may have been required for an additional entrance to the Friars grounds, or for the purpose of gaining access to the River Froom. No better evidence could be obtained of the friendly relations that existed between the townsmen and the Friars than that afforded to us by the fact that the donors of the "toft" were the leading men of the town. Walter Frampton (or Frompton), Elias Spelly, and Thomas Knapp had served as representatives of the town in Parliament and had also respectively served the office of mayor. John Vyell had served as sheriff and mayor. Walter Tidestyle had served as bailiff and M.P. for the town. A translation of the King's License is appended. It will be observed that the Friars had become less scrupulous as to the acquisition of land, which we now find was vested in them "and their successors," in the same form as if they had been a corporate body.

(Extracted from Patent Roll of Richard II., part 1, memb. 25.)

"LICENSE TO GIVE IN MORTMAIN, &c.

"The King to all to whom, &c., greeting. Although, &c., "nevertheless of Our special grace and for 10s. which "Walter Frampton, Elias Spelly, John Vyel, Thomas Knap "and Walter Tidestyle have paid to us we have granted "and given license for us and our heirs as much as in us "lies to the said Walter, Elias, John, Thomas and Walter "that they may give and assign one toft with the "appurtenances in the suburb of Bristol in a certain place "there called the Lewynesmede (near to the house of our "beloved in Christ the warden and convent of the order "of the Friars Minors of Bristol) which is held of us in "burgage to the said warden and convent to hold to them "and their successors towards the increase of the easement "of their said house for ever. And we have likewise by "the tenor of these presents given to the said warden and "convent our special license that they may receive and "hold to them and their successors the said toft with the "appurtenances from the aforesaid Walter, Elias, John, "Thomas and Walter for the increase of the easement of "their said house for ever as is aforesaid notwithstanding "the statute aforesaid or because the said toft is held of us "as is aforesaid We being unwilling that the said Walter, "Elias, John, Thomas and Walter or their heirs or the said "warden and convent or their successors by reason of the "statute aforesaid or of other the premises be disturbed "molested or troubled by us, our heirs, our justices "escheators, sheriffs or other our bailiffs or ministers "whatsoever. Saving nevertheless to us the services of "the said toft due and accustomed. In witness whereof, &c. "Witness the King at Westminster the 16th day of October.
"By w'rnt of Privy Seal"

John Roper, by his will, dated 1390, May 5th, desired to be buried in the Church of the Friars Minors of Bristol if happening to die in the said town or suburb, and testator gave legacies to the four orders of Mendicant Friars there (Bristol Wills).

Adam Frensch (described as "fletcher and burgess") by will, dated 1396, October 12th, desired to be buried in the Church of the Friars Minors of Bristol, beside his late wife, Maud, and testator gave legacies to the said Friars, &c. (Bristol Wills).

Nicholas Hastyng, burgess, by his will, dated 1397, December 3rd, bequeathed to his wife, Margery, a dwellinghouse in Lewynesmede, for her life, on condition of her paying yearly to the Friars Minors and Carmelites of Bristol ijs. vjd. each for their prayers, and also maintaining the taper "cora su'mo Crucifixo" in the Church of St. James, which he "was wont to maintain"—(Bristol Wills).

John Muleward, burgess, by his will, dated 5th June, 1398, bequeathed (inter alia) legacies to the Friars Minors and Carmelites—(Bristol Wills).

Agnes Spelly, whose will was proved 15th May, 1405, desired "to be buried in the Church of the Friars Minors "of Bristol," and she bequeathed a legacy to the Church of St. Leonard at Bristol, in which "her anniversary was to " be duly kept for ever"—(Bristol Wills).

Richard Paans, merchant, by his will, dated 17th Dec., 1406, bequeathed legacies to the Friars Minors and Carmelites. Testator also bequeathed to William Popylton, the Hermit of Rownham, 40 shillings to pray for testator's soul—(Bristol Wills).

Sir William Boneylle, by will of August 13th, 1407, proved March 24th, 1408-9, bequeathed £7 10s. 0d. to the

Austin Friars, the Friars Minors and Friars Preachers of Bristuit (Bristol) £2 10s. 0d. each—(Palmer's "Friar Preachers of Bristol").

Walter Seymour, a "burgess of the town of Bristol," by his will, dated 26th February, 1409, which was proved in the prerogative Court of Canterbury, on the 15th March, 1409, gave 20s. to the Friars, "Item lego ordini frm Minor' "Bristoll xxs."—(P. C. C. Wills).

Alexander Bagenham, by his will, dated 9th February, 1413, gave legacies to the Friars Minors at Oxford and Bristol and Master Peter Russell, "who is to celebrate for testator's soul and the souls of all the faithful dead" (Bristol Wills).

Sir Edmund Seymour, by his will, dated "on the day of "St. Laurence, 1421," gave legacies to the Friars Minors. "Item lego fratribȝ Minoribȝ Bristolł xs. ad distribuend "int' eos singularit' ad celebrand p aia mea in honoȓ "omnium aplor' t sanctor' dei." . . . .
. . . . "Item lego fribȝ Minoribȝ Bristolł xs. ad "distribuend singularit' int' eos ad celebrand pro aia mea in "honore beator Michis t Gabrielis anglor' dei." The will was proved in the Prerogative Court on the 13th June, 1422. (P. C. C. Wills).

Nicholas Bubwith, Bishop of Bath and Wells, Oct. 5th, 1424, bequeathed 50 marks to be distributed among the four Orders of Friars, viz., the Friars Preachers, Minors, Augustinians and Carmelites of London, Ilchester, Bridgwater and Bristol—(Palmer's "Friar Preachers of Bristol").

Thomas Berkeley, described as "burgensis ville Bristollie," by his will, dated 10th April, 1436, proved in the Prerogative Court of Canterbury on the 19th April, 1436, contains bequest to the Friars, "Item lego fribus minoribȝ vilł "Bristoll xxs." This will also contains the following: "Itea "lego quatuor domibȝ elimosināṙ ville Bristoll vjs. viij̇d. "int' eos equalit' dividend."—(P. C. C. Wills).

Lodowic Mors (or Morse), Burgess and Merchant, by his will, dated the 7th February, 1464, amongst other legacies bequeathed certain "pipes of woad in certain ships returning " by the grace of God from parts beyond the seas," and on the happening of certain specified events testator gave " three (pipes) for the reparation of the house of the Friars " Minors of Bristol "—(Bristol Wills).

William Canynges, whose name is immortalized by his good works at St. Mary Redcliffe, was one of the benefactors of the Bristol Franciscans. Barrett (p. 571) quotes a deed relating to the gift of Wm. Canynges to the Convent. The historian, in this case, has added the words " penes me " in his description of the deed.

(Translation of Deed given by Barrett.)

" BE IT KNOWN UNTO ALL MEN, that the 29th day " of November in the year 1465, we the Guardian and " Friars Minor all of the Convent of Bristol there dwelling, " considering the affection of pure devotion of the worshipful " man William Canynges, which he daily shews to the " Order of our Seraphic Father St. Francis and especially " to our Convent aforesaid in exhibiting his alms and " manifold benefits long 'since conferred upon us, and in " future to be bestowed, for out of his pious charity for the " relief of the said Convent he has faithfully given and " paid to the same Convent twenty pounds on the year " and day aforementioned. BY TENOR OF THESE " PRESENTS, with license of Friar Thomas Radnor the " Minister of England, we have promised and granted to " the said William Canynges and Joanna his wife that " their names be inscribed in the gift book (datario) of our " Convent among the chief benefactors of the said Convent, " and that they be recommended as the custom is; and we

"have further promised and granted to the said William
"Canynges and Joanna his wife, that their obit the second
"festival next after St. Peter every year in the Church of
"our said Convent shall be solemnly celebrated with
"exequiis mortuorum and mass of requiem by note for the
"souls of the said William Canynges and Joanna his wife,
"of John Canynges and Joanna his wife, father and mother
"of the said William Canynges, of John Milton and Joanna
"his wife and for the souls for whom it is bound to pray
"and of all the faithful departed, and since from the testimony
"of Christ in the Gospel, the workman is worthy of his
"hire, the aforesaid William, loving his own soul and
"mindful of the words of Christ hath ordained and
"appointed by himself, his heirs and executors to the
"Brothers of the said Convent every year for ever on the
"day aforesaid as well in his lifetime as after his death in
"recompence of their labours, one quarter of an ox of the
"value of forty pence four quarters of a good sheep of the
"price and value of sixteen pence English money and forty
"pence in pure money to be given for bread and ale; that
"therefore the said promise and grant may be so confirmed
"as not to be broken, I Friar Thomas Minister of England
"in virtue of that holy obedience to all the Guardians and
"Friars of the aforementioned Convent present and future
"do command that they solemnly celebrate as well in their
"lifetime as after their death when it comes the exequies
"for the dead with mass of requiem every year on the
"said day for the souls of the said William and Joanna his
"wife and of all the abovementioned, and moreover that
"they cause this to be read in the Chapter House by the
"Friars there gathered together once in the year namely
"on the day or nativity of the Blessed St. Francis. In
"witness of this grant and promise the Seal of my Office

"together with the Seal of the Keeper of the Custody of
"Bristol and Convent of Bristol is openly appended. Done
"read and sealed at Bristol before the Friars of the afore-
"mentioned Convent in their Chapter House met the day
"and year above written."

William Canynges, by his will, dated 12th Nov., 1474, gave (amongst a number of gifts for lights, torches, tapers, masses, &c.) "To the Order of Friars Minors of Bristol "xx^{li}, on condition of their being at the mortuary offices and "mass on the day of burial, and of the month's mind, in "the aforesaid Church of Redcliff, and on the day of the "anniversary in the first year after testator's death." [Testator is described in the will as "Clerk, Dean of the "Collegiate Church and College of the Holy Trinity of "Westbury-upon-Trym, by Bristol, in the Diocese of "Worcester, and lately a Merchant of the Town of Bristol."] (Bristol Wills.)

Richard Hatter, burgess and merchant of Bristol, by will, dated 5th September, 1457, made the following bequests:—
"Item lego ffratrib3 Minorib3 Bristollie venientib3 et "infessentib3 ad dirḡ t missam meam et ad orandum "spialiter pro anima mea xxs. Item lego tribus aliis "ordinibus fratrum mendicancium Bristollie ibidem existen' "eodem modo videlicet cuilibet ordini eorum xiijs. iiijd."— [Proved in the Prerogative Court on the 21st Sept., 1457.]

Thomas Rowley, a burgess and merchant of Bristol, by his will, dated 11th January, 1478, which was proved in the Prerogative Court of Canterbury on the 25th February, 1478, bequeathed the following sums for religious purposes:—
"Lego corpus meum sepeliend in ecclia pochiali sancti'
"Johannis Baptiste ville Bristoll in eodem loco ubi modo
"jacet corpus Walteri Frampton quondam burgens̄ ville
"p̄dict̄. Lego ad sustentacionem Cantarie dei Walti fframpton

"in dēā ecclesia centum libras ad inveniend duos Capellanos
"divina celebrant ibm ad altare bte Marie impptm. (If the
"parishioners of the said Church do not find the said
"chaplains, then the said £100 shall be divided and the
"4 orders of the 'fratrum mendicanciũ Bristollie' shall
"have £20 to be equally divided amongst them). . . . .
"Item lego ordini frm minorum Bristoll xls. Item lego
"ceteris tribus ordinibus frm mendicanciũ Bristoll cuilibet
"eoȝ xxs. Item lego dc̃e ecclesie sancti Johannis post
"decessum Margarete uxoris mee unũ missale," etc.—(P.C.C.
Wills).

[NOTE.—In connection with the Chatterton forgeries it
will be remembered that "Turgot's Account of Bristol" was
alleged to have been translated from the original Saxon
"by Thomas Rowlie, parish preeste of St. John's in the city
"of Bristol, in the year 1465." There seems to be very
little doubt that Chatterton borrowed the name from a
tombstone or document in St. John the Baptist Church. The
Rowley family appear to have been connected with the
parish for several generations.]

Edward Dawes, merchant, by will, dated July 21st, 1493,
proved at Lambeth, August 6th, 1493, gave legacies "to
"the prior or guardian and convent of each house of mendi-
"cant friars in Bristol."

The will of Robert Thorne, dated the 17th May, 1532, and
proved the 10th October, 1532, contains a bequest of "The
"sum of £20 to each of the four orders of friars in
"Bristowe, the one half for the reparation of their churches
"and houses, and the other for their sustentation."

[NOTE.—In only rare instances the legacy exceeded
twenty shillings—Thorne (one of the founders of the
Grammar School) was a very rich man.]

Records of gifts to the four orders of friars are to be
found in a very large number of wills proved at Bristol, but

it would serve no good purpose to add to the fairly representative specimens of gifts by will which have been quoted. For the sake of illustration some further examples of bequests to the Friars will be found in the next chapter.

The Rev. C. F. R. Palmer, in the course of his exhaustive researches anent the history of the Friars Preachers, met with a considerable number of wills of Bristol burgesses, merchants, mariners, etc., of the fourteenth, fifteenth and early sixteenth centuries, in the registers of the Prerogative Court of Canterbury, which contain legacies to each of the four orders of friars in Bristol for prayers, masses, placebos, etc.; and bequests to them appear in the wills of some Bristol townsmen (who were probably residents of the parishes of Temple, St. Mary Redcliff or St. Thomas) which were proved in the Consistory Court of Wells.

It was an almost universal custom in Bristol for testators to bequeath, either with or without a condition, a small legacy to each of the four Orders of Friars. The formal wording of the bequests varies so little that one is unconsciously led to the conclusion that at some time or other those to whom were entrusted the preparation of the wills of the townsmen must have come to an understanding to advise the testators to place the four Orders on the same terms. Some, in fact most, of these legacies were very insignificant in amount, but the Friars were dependent on alms to a considerable extent, and these small bequests probably came to be regarded as "unconsidered trifles," which at times must have proved very useful to them. Some of the gifts to them were in kind, as for example, "also every Frere (Friar) in every House of the iiij. Orders "of Bristowe shall have a lofe," which was the form of an annual dole from the Abbey of St. Augustine on the occasion of the anniversary of Robert Fitzharding, the founder—(Newland's Chronicle), and, as a further example, Stephen Forster, of Bristol, merchant, by his will, gave a measure of woad "of vj. m're warantise" to every house of "the iiij. ordres of ffreres in Bristowe to pray for my good "fryndes and me"—(Bristol Wills, No. 288).

. . . .

The following wills of persons, other than Bristol townsmen, contain small legacies to each of the four orders of Friars of Bristol :—

(PREROGATIVE COURT WILLS.)

NAME.	DATE OF WILL.	REGISTER.
Alice West, Lady of Hynton	25 July,	1395 (Rous, fol. 29[b])
Thomas Tanner, of Wells	23 Nov.,	1401 (Marche, fol. 11)
John Ken, of Ken	9 Nov.,	1404 (Marche, fol. 56)
John Wytloff, Rector of Lodiswell	2 April,	1405 (Marche, fol. 65[b])
Edward Curteys, of Wells	Oct.,	1413 (Marche, fol. 222)
Richard Clerk, of Pennysford	6 Feb.,	1415 (Marche, fol. 224[b])
William Chapman, of Mersfield	10 March,	1416 (Marche, fol. 296[b])
Sir Richard Chokke, of Long Ashton	3 July,	1483 (Logge, fol. 163[b])
Dame Margaret Chokke (widow)	1 Sept.,	1483 (Logge, fol. 70)
Thomas Tripnell, of Magna Childefelde	5 Nov.,	1487 (Milles, fol. 57[b])
John Tyndescy, Clerk ("at Westbury")	1 Oct.,	1487 (Milles, fol. 187[b])
John Compton, of Bekynton	19 July,	1503 (Holgrave)
John Rose, of Frome Selwode	24 Jan.,	1510 (Holgrave)

Chapter III.

WE have seen that the four Orders of Friars were very frequently placed on equal terms by the will makers of the period, but in various other ways they were treated on terms of equality, and a benevolent neutrality towards them generally seems to have been the attitude of the townsmen; consequently, it is almost impossible to enter into the history of one of the four Orders without treading on ground that is common to all. In the Pre-Reformation period of the History of Bristol all the Friars were much in evidence in everyday life; they were to be found in the imposing and picturesque processions through the streets with the trade Guilds, in which pictorial and living representations of the religious and secular communities were harmoniously blended; and they were also to be found in the squalid homes of the poorer townsmen in attendance on the sick and needy. A townsman, by his will, frequently made manifest his partiality towards them by making provision for the presence of representatives of each Order at his funeral to celebrate the mortuary offices and to say masses, on which occasion they sometimes received "bread, cheese and ale" in addition to a small legacy. Robert May of Bristol by his will, dated 29th August, 1395, bequeathed to each order of Mendicant Friars of Bristol "30 pence for a trental to be sung for my soul" (Bristol Wills, No. 74). [A trental consisted of thirty masses, rehearsed for thirty days successively.] Henry

London bequeathed twenty shillings to be equally divided amongst the four orders of Mendicant Friars "for the celebration of four trentals" (Bristol Wills, No. 56). Another townsman made provision "for the "celebration," by the four orders, of "forty trentals in "their churches" (Bristol Wills, No. 67). It was also of frequent occurrence to provide for the "month's mind" and the "year's mind." A specimen of the form of bequest is here given. The will of Margaret Gerves, the widow of Simon Gerves, "Toker," of Bristol, dated 20th December, 1530, contains the following legacy—" To " the IIII orders " of fryers in Bristowe so that they be at my burial, month-" mynd, and yere-mynd xls. (equally)".—(Wells Wills).

Occasionally the Friars were directed by a special clause in the will to say "dirige" and mass in their own churches in lieu of their attendance at the testator's funeral. There are to be found instances of money given for the establishment in perpetuity of an obit or anniversary service for the souls of deceased persons. During the fourteenth century many Chantries were founded in Bristol by wealthy townsmen, and the will or deed by which the Chantry was established contained a declaration or trust that the endowment should be vested in or be under the control of the Corporation. From "Spicer's Obit" (one of several "obits" vested in the Commonalty of Bristol) the four Orders of Friars were entitled to receive yearly from the Corporation 13^s. 4^d. The Sheriff's Accounts for the year 1517 include an item which proves that the Friars were recognised by the Corporation. "Item to the iiij. " ordres of freres xxxijs." (MSS. British Museum). That this was an annual payment is testified by an entry in the Great White Book of the Corporation relating to the year 1520, from which it appears that each of the four Orders of Friars received 8/-, making a total of 32/-, which corresponds with the payments to them in the accounts relating to the year 1517. There cannot be any doubt as to the existence of friendly recognition and intercourse between the Friars and the townsmen for several centuries. "Ricart's "Kalendar," which is one of the most valuable MS. records preserved at the Council House, contains an account of the ancient usages of the Corporation. It is therein set forth that "The Maire and Shiref of Bristowe shall . . . . . " kepe their Advent Sermondes . . . . . . at which "furst Sonday (of Advent) the seide Maire and Shiref, with "theire brethern shall walke to the Ffrere Preachours [the "Black Friars] and there hyre (hear) their Sermonde. And "the next Sonday thereupon they shall hyre (hear) "Sermonde at the Ffrere Menors [the Gray Friars], and the "thirde Sonday at the Ffrere Preachers, and the fourthe "and laste Sonday of Advent at the Ffrere Menors."

The friendly feeling shewn by the townsmen and Corporation towards the Friars apparently continued down to the date of the dissolution: but it is more than probable that for a considerable time prior to the King's resolve to suppress their establishments there had been a gradual falling off in the alms bestowed by the townsmen upon them. A perusal of the letters of the Commissioners sent by the King to obtain the surrender of the various houses of Mendicant Friars throughout the country will prove that in Bristol and elsewhere all or nearly all the houses were in debt, and that some of them were hopelessly insolvent. It is true that in a very few cases the provincial houses were fairly well endowed, but these were exceptions to the general rule. A careful study of the history of the English Franciscans will satisfy any unprejudiced mind that it was rarely indeed that they were the owners of anything beyond their houses and the gardens, &c., belonging thereto. It will be seen hereafter that, at the date of the dissolution, the four establishments in Bristol were comparatively small ones. Their bad financial condition at this period may have been partly due to the fact that money was not over plentiful, and the Friars probably suffered in consequence of the curtailment of the means of their patrons and friends; and it must not be forgotten that it was well known to the townsmen that the dissolution of their houses was at hand. That they had been regarded by the clergy with other than friendly feelings is a well-known historical fact, but it is hard to imagine that this prevented them from pursuing the even tenor of their way without disquietude or alarm. Their poverty would have afforded the only good reason for any anxiety, because it is certain that the townsmen of Bristol were at no time antagonistic to them, and, down to the very last, the Friars were still named in their wills as the recipients of small legacies. But, notwithstanding their long run of popularity, it must not be supposed that they were always permitted to be free from those attacks which, deservedly or undeservedly, are made at some time or other on nearly all individuals and institutions. The first important attack was made by the "Lollards," who were amongst the earliest advocates of reform in Church doctrine and practice in England. Towards the latter part of the fourteenth century Wickliff and his followers were actively engaged in preaching in favour of certain changes; and, although the crusade was directed in general terms, it seems clear that the Mendicant Friars came in for more than a fair share of abuse.

John Purveye, or **Purnay**, who was Wickliff's curate or assistant, preached at Bristol; and his sermons may be taken as fairly representative of the style of advocacy adopted by the Lollard preachers. Knighton says, 'This John Purveye, "like the rest of them, always in his sermons very much "commended his own partizans, but always and everywhere "he openly reviled those who were not so with pernicious "abuse, *particularly the Mendicants*," also that the Lollard preachers were "*continually reviling the Mendicant* "*Friars, calling them false brothers.*"

The three celebrated sermons preached by Latimer in Bristol form a link in the chain of circumstances directly connected with the Reformation. The first sermon was preached on the Second Sunday in Lent, 1534, at St. Nicholas' Parish Church, in the forenoon; his second in the Black Friars (the Dominicans), in the afternoon, and the third on the following day (Monday), in the parish church of St. Thomas. Hubberden, the champion of the Papists and Latimer's uncompromising opponent, subsequently visited Bristol, "and preached yn Saynte Thomas Chyrche at "after none on Ester eve and at Saynte Nycholas Chyrche "before noon on Ester day, and there preched scharply "aganste Latomers Artycules"—(MS. Cotton. Cleo. E iv., fol. 56).

The two disputants had evidently caused much commotion in the town, and the matter having been brought to the King's notice, he appointed certain Commissioners to ascertain by written and *vivâ voce* evidence what statements were made by the two over-zealous preachers in their sermons. The Commissioners opened the enquiry on Sunday, the 5th day of July, 1534, at St. James's Priory. Amongst other matters put before the Commissioners anent this controversy occurs the following:—"Also that same "Sonday one Gylberte Cogan came to the howse of the "Gray Fryers in Bristow, and said to the warden of the

"same howse that he schowlde beware what he scholde
"wryte and testyfy, for there schowlde cume iiije. that
"*schowlde testify the contrary*, as the seyde warden
"shewyd hyt manyfestely before all the commyssyoners"
(MS. Cotton. Cleo. E 4, fol. 56).

[NOTE.—"Gylbert Cogan" was Sheriff of Bristol for the year 1522.]

Another link in the chain of circumstances was the gross imposture and conspiracy in the year 1533, in which Elizabeth Barton (the so-called "Holy Maid" of Kent) was put forward as the instrument of deception. One of the pretended visions of the "Holy Maid" contained a suggestion *(probably based on an actual fact)* that the King had contemplated marriage with Anne Boleyn ("his favourite "lady") at Calais, in October of the previous year, on the occasion of his visit to the French King. In a description of the "visions," in MS. Cotton. Cleo. E iv., fol. 75, there are no less than thirty matters or prophecies referred to.

In the "Letters relating to the suppression of Monasteries" it is said "that some of the Friars Observants (Franciscans) "of Richmond and Greenwich participated largely in the "conspiracy." Amongst the names of those hanged at Tyburn, on the 10th April, 1534, for participation in the affair, appear those of Hugh Rich, Warden of the Canterbury (Franciscan) Friars, and Richard Risby, who held a similar official position at Richmond. It will be seen hereafter that at the date of the dissolution of the Bristol Convent the Warden thereof was also Warden of the Convent at Richmond (see p. 79.) This Warden's name is given at p. 87. It cannot be doubted that the Franciscans were zealous and bold defenders of the Papal authority, and took a prominent part in forming popular opinion against the King, whose unscrupulous and despicable conduct in obtaining from a slavish parliament a declaration involving the illegitimacy of his daughter, Mary, was calculated to arouse their just indignation. These Friars were not the least shrewd of the religious orders, and their poverty probably emboldened them in their opposition to the King's desires. Their train of thought must have been filled with the knowledge that they had no valuable possessions which the King could take from them as a penalty for their obstinacy. But, however shrewd they may have been, it is impossible to imagine that it ever entered into their calculations that their proceedings would end in the decisive step afterwards taken by the King. Those who have carefully read the history of the Reformation will remember that it was a Franciscan Friar, named Peto (Warden of the Observants of Greenwich), who openly reprimanded the King in rather coarse language touching his marriage in a sermon preached in the King's presence, on the 1st day of May, 1534.* On the 15th day of June Bishop Lee and Thomas Bedyll, on the King's behalf, made an unsuccessful attempt to induce the *Warden and Convent* of Richmond and the *Convent* of Greenwich (Peto, the *Warden*, had probably been sent away before this) to subscribe to a declaration of the King's supremacy over the Papal authority (MS. Cotton Cleo. E iv., fol. 10). The refusal of these Friars to subscribe to this declaration must be treated as one of the most important events leading up to the dissolution of the religious houses, and it is certain that it precipitated the impending crash. On the 11th August the King gave " the first blow " to the Franciscans by expelling the Friars of Greenwich from their house, and the same fate very shortly afterwards befel other Convents. Here we must pass over the interval that elapsed before the actual dissolution of the four houses of Mendicant Friars in Bristol took place.

* There is a little doubt as to the exact day when this incident happened.

It was intended, when this Collectanea was in course of formation, to confine it strictly to facts relating to the Friars Minors, but when it became apparent that it would be possible to give something like a complete story of the circumstances connected with the dissolution of the four houses of Mendicant Friars in Bristol, which information was in part common to all, it was thought desirable to depart to a certain extent from the original purpose in order that the details of the history of the fate of all the Bristol houses of Mendicants might be included.

The house of the Carmelites was the first of the Bristol houses of the Mendicants given up to the King. In a letter to Secretary Cromwell from Richard, Suffragan Bishop of Dover, (one of the Commissioners appointed by the King in the suppression of religious houses), which contains no date, but which was probably written in the month of July, 30, Henry VIII. (1538), the King's Commissioner (euphemistically styled " The Visitor ") said, " Sythe that I "last wroght to yower lordschype I have received iiij. howsys " into the King's hands." [The Bristol Carmelites was one of the four houses he had just taken possession of, the three other houses were situated in the town of Gloucester.] He then adds the following description of the Carmelite house :—" The White Fryeres in Bristowe, the whyche all " that was in yt ys lytyll more than payd the dettes. Yt " is a goodly howse in byldenge, mete for a great man, no " renttes but ther gardens. There ys a chapell and an yle " off the Church, and dyverse gutteres, spowtes and condytes " lede [of lead], the rest all tylle and slate. A goodly laver " and condyte(*) comynge to yt. Thys howse was in dett " above xvj^{li}, of the whyche paid viij^{li}, the rest discharged " by plegeys [pledges]." It also appears that the house was put into safe custody until the King's pleasure " be

(*) See p.p. 78, 79, 98.

"further knowyn" (MS. Cotton. Cleop. E iv., fol. 251). There was no formal surrender in writing in the usual form, but the following statement or declaration, signed by four of the Friars in the presence of the Mayor of Bristol, will explain how their house passed into the hands of the King's Commissioner:—

EXCH. TREA. OF RECEIPT. VOL. B $\frac{2}{19}$ F. 19.

"M^d thys xxviij. day of Julii in y^e xxx. yere of Kyng
"Hery the viij^{te} Rychard byshop of Dovor & vesytor for the
"Kynges grace beyng in brystow browte before the meyar
"ther iiij. ffreers late of y^e wheyte freers ther the whyche
"cōfessyd before the seyd meyar that they volūtaryly
"dede leve ther howse in brystow be cause they pseyveyd
"that they before had dyu'se p^{l}ors the whyche had sold
"and pluneyd all ye jewells and substans wth ye oder
"ornamets & stuffe of that howse & yett lefte them in dett
"& no thyng to leve wth and also cosyderyng that y^e
"charyte of the pepull ys very small so that they cannott
"se how to cotynew & leve in ther howse wherfore
"volu'taryly they gyffe ther howse in to ye vesytors handds
"to ye Kyngs vse they also ther cōfessyd that ye seyd
"vesytor had gyffe to them all ther owyn chambers & all
"ye boks of the quere & dyu'se order small inplemets &
"eche of them a lett^r & xx^d in ther purseys to bryng
"them to ther couētry & gayff them c'ten tymys to vesyte
"ther fryndds & so he hathe wth ij. onest men of the towne
"p^{r}seyd all ye moveabulls & payd ye chargys and old detts
"& made a pfyte inuētory of the stuff that ys leffe the
"custody of yt wth the howse in the handds of John Mereke.

"per me ffr̄ Thomē Clyfton subp^{r}orem [1]
"p me fr̄ Thomā Wraxall.
"p me fr̄ Symō Wagon (or Vagan). [2]
"p me fr̄ Johm Hop"(er) [3]

(1) The Prior had probably disappeared.
(2) The signature is almost illegible.
(3) Subsequently permission to "change their apparel" was applied for on behalf of these four Friars.

It will be seen by the following copy of the inventory of the Carmelite's house that the King's Commissioner peremptorily sold the whole of the goods and chattels found in it, with the exception of the articles handed by him to the Friars and "ij. chales" and "ij. bells." It appears by the letter or report as to this house from the Commissioner to Secretary Cromwell that, in consequence of "the gret clamor that was for dettes there," the Commissioner had applied to the Mayor to appoint men to appraise the goods, and that he had sold them in order to satisfy the importunate creditors. This was a somewhat unusual state of things, because, although it was ascertained with regard to other houses that they were in bad circumstances, yet the sale of a small portion of the goods and chattels sufficed, as a rule, to pay the debts, and in the end there was something in the way of money or money's worth (sometimes a not inconsiderable sum, especially in places where articles of silver were in use) to be handed over. His Majesty "the pious Monarch" and "defender of "the faith," whom we may fairly describe as the Champion religious hypocrite of the period, was particularly keen on the articles of silver, the lead, and the embroidered copes, &c.

"The Invētory of Bristow yͤ Whyte Freers.
[First four lines are blank.]
" Item a sute of mare maydys pryst decon and
    " subdecon   -   -   - xiij^s
" Item a decon and subdecon blewe -   - x^s
" Item a whyte sute wth lyons pryst decō and
    " subdecō -   -   -   - xvj^s
" Item a blacke sute pryst decō and subdecō - iij^s iiij^d
" Item a sylke cope wth byrde -   - v^s
" Item ij. grene cope of sylke   -   - v^s
" Item ij. vyolet coops strypys sylke -   - iiij^s
" Item v. old coopys   -.   -   - viij^s
" Item v. cheasabuls   -   -   - v^s

"Item v. tunakylls	-	iij˙	
"Item a herse clothe	-	-	xvjᵈ
"Item an aultʳ clothe	-	-	viijᵈ
"Item a vaylle	-	-	viijᵈ
"Item an albe	-	-	vjᵈ
"Item a table clothe	-	-	vjᵈ
"Item a piece of a cope	-	-	xijᵈ
"Item ij. curteyns and an altʳ frunte	-	viijᵈ
"Item ij. fetherbedds	-	xiij˙	iijᵈ
"Item x. cusheyns	-	iij˙	iiijᵈ
"Item ij. baasons and ane ewer	-	iij˙	iiijᵈ
"Item iiij. platters and iij. pottyngers	-	iij˙	iiijᵈ
"Item ij. panys	-	ij˙	
"Item iij. potts	-	xˢ	
"Item ij. chests	-	-	xvjᵈ
"Item a lyttyll table	-	-	viijᵈ
"Item a cubborde	-	iij˙	
"Item ij. olde carpetts	-	-	vjᵈ
"Item olde hangyngs of yᵉ qwere	-	-	xvjᵈ
"Item a forme	-	-	iiijᵈ
"Item a tester and a syler grene say-	-	xijᵈ
"Item hangyngs of grene saye	-	-	xijᵈ
"Item a bedstede	-	-	xijᵈ
"Item a lyttyll cobborde	-	-	iiijᵈ
"Item a table a payr of trystyls and a forme	-	xijᵈ
"Item v. joynyd stoolys	-	-	xvjᵈ
"Item hangyngs of the qwere doruyxe	-	xvjᵈ
"Item an old vestyment of sattyn brygges	-	vˢ	
"Item ij. awndyryns	-	-	xxᵈ
"Item a steynyd clothe	-	-	vjᵈ
"Item a chayre and a coffer	-	-	xiijᵈ
"Item a bedstede	-	-	xᵈ
"Item a tabull and ij. trystyls	-	-	iiijᵈ

"Item a fetherbed and ij. bolster - - vj^s viij^d
"Item a chayre and a cheste -' - xij^d
"Item a copur to brew wythe - - xij^d
"Item a brasse pott - - - xvj^d
"Item a platt^r and a saucer - - vj^d
"Item a dowble barre w^t ij. hangels - - v^d
"Item a lyttylle carderon - - - vj^d
"Item iij. brooches - - - xx^d
"Item ij. racks - - - - iij^s
"Item iij. barrys standyng in ye wall - x^d
"Item a trevet a payr of tongs aud a fryeng pan xviij^d
"Item ij. busshl of whete - - - xij^d
"Item a baasyn and a platter - - xij^d
"Item a lampe in the quere - - vj^d
"Item in ye sextrye old chests - - xx^d

    "Sue viij^{li} ij^s xj^d

"Ther be ij. chales coper the wheche ye^e vesyter hathe.
"The be ij. bells the wheche the meyer and evans schall se
 "ye sale of them.
"The house is in the handds of [blank] evans at ye vesyter
 "and meyers assynemeut to se it orderyd tyll y^e kyngs
 "pleser be further knowyn.
"Of y^e money above wrytyn was payde as by
 "y^e accountts it schall appere - - viij^{li} ij^s j^d
"So restytht in my hands - - x^d
"And ij. cop chales. For sylu^r there was nō.

      "Ricard Doverēes."

  (*Exch. Tre. of Receipt, Vol. A $\frac{3}{11}$, fo. 47.*)

There are no remains of the White Friars buildings, which stood on or contiguous to the site of the Colston Hall. The Friars' gardens were extensive, and well situated for culture. To these Friars the parishioners of St. John's parish were under deep obligation for the gift of a never-failing supply of pure water, which still exists, and is the common property of the inhabitants. Let us pay "the "passing tribute of a sigh" to the memory of the good Friars for the inestimable boon they conferred on the townsmen. A description of, and references to, the White Friars conduit will be found at p.p. 98, 99, and 100.

In a subsequent report from the King's Commissioner to Secretary Cromwell, dated "thys xxvij. day of August" (1538), references were made to the three other Bristol houses of Mendicant Friars, "Also there be iij. convents y^t " in Bristowe, as for the Blacke [the Dominicans] [they] be " redy to give up, but the other ij. be styffe and bere them " sore be gret favor. The Gray Fryeres *by reason that the* "*warden ys warden of Rechemonde*, and ys in favor by " reson of that, yet for all hys grett port I thynke him " xx. merkes [marks] in dett, and not abull to pay yt. The " Austen Fryer by reson of a grantt that he hathe of the " King's grace for the terme of hys lyffe, by the whyche he " thynketh that he may sell the howse and all, for the " plate ys all solde, and allso the tymber that grene abowte " the howse, so that he hath within iij. yeres taken above a " hunderyd markes of plate and tymber and other imple-" ments, so that almost all ys gon: If it wolde plese you " to send yower plesur by this brynger of theys ij. conventes " in Brystowe, in my cumynge home I shall cum within " x. myle of Brystowe, and so I would thether to fynysche " all thoys partes, and so I wolde to Salysbury and other " ther, yf that I knewe yower plesur"—(MS. Cotton. Cleop, E iv., fol. 263).

The Commissioner returned to Bristol in the month of September (1538), and, on or about the tenth of that month, he obtained possession of the three remaining houses of Mendicant Friars, viz.:—The Austins, The Dominicans (Black), and Franciscans (Gray), as the following copies of the surrenders will testify. A copy of the inventory of the goods and chattels of each of the three houses will be found after the respective surrenders.

(Copy Surrender of The Austin Friars.)

"M^d we ye p'or & cōuente of ye austen fryers of brystow
"w^t owt any man^r of coaceyon or cōsell do gyue ow^r howse
"in to ye handds of ye lorde vysytor to the Kings use
"desyerynge hys grace to be goode & gracyows to us. In
"wyttenes we subscrybe ow^r namys w^t ow^r pper handds
"the x. day of September in ye xxx^th yere of ye raygne of
"ow^r most drede sou^en lorde Kynge Henry ye viii^th.

"p nos v̄ 5.
"p me frēm Nichm Sandford p'orem.
"p me frēm Johem Ingman.
"p me frēz Laureciū Frakys.
"p me frēz Johane Stere.
"p me frēz Johez Pynder.
"p me frēz Thomā P'ker.
"p me frēm Rogerū Fylyon.
"p me frēz Robertū P'fey."

(Copy Inventory of The Austin Friars.)

"This indenture makith mencyon of all suche stuffe of
"the austen freres of bristow receyuyd by the lorde visetor
"vnder the lorde p'uey seale for the Kingis grace the w^ch
"ys holly delyu'erd to Harry White of bristow grocer and
"Will'm popley gentilman to order and saffly kepe the
"same to the Kingis vse, till the Kingis plesure shall be
"further knowen w^t ye place and all the appten^ncs.

"The Vestre.

"ffirst vestmentes for prist decon and subdecon of blewe
  "saten browdered w^t aubis and chesebille and a cope
  "of ye same.
"Item vestments for prist decon and subdecon of change-
  "abill sarcenet poudred w^t starrys of golld w^t on cope
  "of same.
"Item vestments for prist decon and subdecon of blew
  "sarcenet.
"Item vestments for prist decon and sbdecon of change-
  "bill silke brodered w^t flowerys w^t on cope of the
  "same.
"Item vestments for prist decon and sbdecon of bawdkin.
"Item iiij. copes of diu^{r}se colorys embrouderyd.
"Item ij. vestments of redde veluit w^t on aube.
"Item a vestment of white damaske.
"Item a cope of blacke damaske.
"Item xij. vestments of diu^{r}se sortis of dornix fustan & say.
"Item iij. pelowys for ye alt^r of linin clothe wrowte w^t silk.
"Item ij. alt^r clothes.
"Item iij. litill cotis for scinthe sethe.
"Item a bann^r for ye crosse of damaske w^t imagis peynted
  "w^t golld.
"Item a gret peyer of laten candlestickis and ij. peyer of
  "small.
"Item a branche of laten afore scinthe austen.
"Item a peyer organys.
"Item a case to put vestments in.

"The Hall.

"Item a tabill and a peyer of trestellys and ij. olld tabill
  "clotheis on all to rent.
"Item in the litill hall a tabill and a peyer of trestles.

F

"THE KECHIN.

"Item a gret pot, ij. posnetis and a broken pott.
"Item iij. pannys, a chafer, and on chaffin dishe.
"Item on long broche and iij. litill brocheis w^t a small pair
  "of rackis.
"Item xvij. pecis of peut^r on and other.
"Item a treuit and a gridiron.
"Item a laten bason and a fier pike.
"M^d the visitor hathe to ye Kingis vse a chales weyng
"xj. vnc g^t, and no peny for his costis, and where y^r ys
"demaunded of true detts about ye su^n of ix. or x^{li} for
"payement w^{r}of ys solld a crucifeix and iij. mass bandis of
"silu^r veing xvij. vnc for ye wch ys receyued towardis y^e
"detts iiij. marks vj^s ij^d and for the payment of ye rest yt
"ys appoyntid y^t certeyne leade y^t was conveyd and sū
"other thingis at y^e sethe of them y^t haue y^e howse in
"keping schall be solld and the dettis y^{r}with to be payde,
"also y^e euidens and writings of y^t howse be left w^t y^e
"inventory.
    "p me Harry White.
    "p me Willm popley."
(Exch. Trea. of Rec, Vol. B $\frac{2}{19}$, fo. 115.)

Leland says, "The Augustine Friers house was harde by "the Temple Gate within it Northe Weste." They have left no name in the district formerly occupied by them as the site of their house and gardens, and not a vestige of their buildings can now be seen. So far as the general public are concerned, the name of the Austin Friars of Bristol is an utter blank, and consequently the Friars are frequently confused with the **Augustinian** Black Canons of the Abbey (now the Cathedral). Comparatively few of the inhabitants of Temple parish are aware that the parishioners in old times were indebted to the Austin Friars for a supply of pure water. The conduit stood near the Friars' house at Temple Gate, and the water was subsequently conveyed from there by a pipe to the Temple cross. These Friars were known as the Order of "Eremites" (Hermits), but their popular designation was "The Austins."

[NOTE.—Inasmuch as references have been made to the conduits of the other three orders of Friars, it has been thought desirable to give some details as to the Temple conduit, and the same will be found at p. p. 102—105].

It is now proposed to give a copy of the surrender of the Black Friars. If a comparison is made of this and the surrender of the Austins, it will be seen that they are in precisely similar form, and dated the same day. A copy of the inventory follows after the surrender.

(COPY SURRENDER OF THE BLACK FRIARS.)

"M^d We ye p'or and co'uente of ye blackefryers of "Brystowe w^t one assent and co'sent w'owt any man' of "cooceyon or co'sell do gyve in to ye handds of ye lorde "vysytor to ye Kyngs vse desyerynge hys grace to be "good and gracyous to vs. In wyttenes we subscrybe "ow^r namys w^t ow^r p'per handds ye x. day of September in "ye xxx^{te} yere of ow^r most dred sou'en lord Kinge Henry "ye VIIIth.

    "Thom^s Paerker, p'or.
    "Rob'tus Wellys.
    "Jacobus Zarman.
    "Wyll'm Garnar.
    "Radulfus Doole."

(Copy Inventory of the Black Friars.)
"The Blacke Fryers of Brystowe.

"Thys Ind't' makeythe me'cyon of all ye stuffe of y^e
"blacke fryers of Brystowe receywed by ye lorde vysyte^r
"vnd' the lorde p'vy seale for the Kyngs grace and
"delyu'ed to Robarde Wodwarde and John Amerke to se
"and order to ye Kyngs vse w^t ye howe and all the
"porten'nce tyll the Kyngs plesur be forther knowyn.

"The Q'r.

"Item a payer of gret candelsteks laten.
"Item a small payer of candelstks laten.
"Item a fayer hangeynge lomps.
"Item a payer of organs.
"Item a holy wat' stope.

"The^{re} Sextre.

"Item in p'mis xvj. copys.
"Item iiij. sutys of grene.
"Item iij. sutys of blewe.
"Item a sute of whyte.
"Item xij. syngle vesteme'ts w^t ther albs.
"Item xiiij. amys for copys.
"Item a payer of red curtens.
"Item a payer of whyte and on' grene curten.
"Item iij. payer of small curtens.
"Item a rede hangeynge.
"Item a whyte and a grene for ye hey aut^r.
"Item ij. rede frengys.
"Item ij. a whyte and a grene.
"Item ij. towels wrowght w^t sylke.
"Item iiij. surplyseys and ij. lytyll rocketts for chyldren.

"Item vj. aut' clothes.
"Item ix. hangyngs for y⁵ low aut'rs.
"Item xv. cop'as casys.
"Item a vayle clothe.
"Item a clothe of sylke to hange befor y⁵ hey aut'.
"Item ij. canapys for y⁵ sacrame't.
"Item ij. pawls for y⁵ q're.
"Item iij. cuschyngs for y⁵ hey aut'.
"Item for y⁵ crosse one of veluet.
"Item a nother of sylke.
"Item for y⁵ aut'rs in lent xxij. clotheys to cou' the' and y⁵
 "ymagys.
"Item a corten of lynyn to draw before y⁵ aut'.
"Item a pawle for y⁵ herse.
"Item ij. peynteyd clothes of kyngs and a nother of marys.
"Item a crane for copys.
"Item a brode for copys.
"Item v. coffers good and bade.

"The Chambers.

"Item iij. fether beds w' iij. bolsters.
"Item ij. cou'yngs.
"Item iij. towells vj. napkyns.
"Item iij. chayers iij. carpetts.
"Item ij. playne tabulls a cow't'.
"Item ij. cupbords.
"Item a gret payer of anndyorns.
"Item a lytyll payer.
"Item a bason and an ewer w' a lytyll bason.
"Item iiij. gret ca'delsteks w' a lytyll ca'dellsteke.
"Item a hangynge of whyte for a bede.
"Item iij. pewt' pots to put flowers in.
"Item ij. quart potts pewt'.

"THE KECHYN.

"Item iiij. gret brasse potts and ij. lytyll potts w^t a
"possenet.
"Item a ketell and a lytyll pan.
"Item a brasyn mort' w^t a pastell.
"Item a chaffer v. broches ij. hengells.
"Item a payer of racks.
"Item a gret charg^r v. plat's vj. dysches of pewt'.
"Item vj. potyngers vj. sawcers of one sort.
"Item vj platers vj. dysches and v. sawcers iij. co't' fetis.
"Item a treuet and a gredyron.
"M^d Y^e vysytor hath w^t him to y^e Kyngs vse ij. chales
"a sensor a brokyn crosse w^t stonys and ycorn in y^t a
"paxse and ij. ca'delstcks all weynge as y^t ys $_{\text{viij}}^{\text{xx}}$. and
"xvj. vnc' and yt ys to be noteyd y^t ther was solde a
"vestemet w^t deco' and subdeco' and one olde syngle
"vesteme't w^t ij. copys for vi^{li} xvj^s viij^d w^t the whyche
"ali detts wer payd and a cou'ynge for xx^s peyseys seleyd
"and ij. vnseleyd and x. patents all in a casket. Also
"xiij. peyseys seleyd in a nother boxse.
"p^r me Robertu' Wodwarde.
"p' me John Amerycke."

(Exch. Treas. of Receipt, Vol. A $\frac{3}{11}$).

The fact that some of the buildings of the Black Friars (including the dormitory, an unique specimen of its kind, and which possesses almost a national reputation) still remain has directed attention to the site of this house, and consequently considerable interest has been taken with regard to its history by archæologists and antiquaries, in whose publications descriptions of the remains have been given on several occasions..

After the dissolution the site of the house of the Black Friars was sold by the King, in the year 1540, to William Chester, who had served the office of mayor in the year 1538. The site of the Friars' house, gardens, &c., now belongs to the Society of Friends, upon a portion of which their Chapel stands, and it is a somewhat curious fact to relate that the locus in quo is very generally known in modern parlance as "The Quakers' Friars"!*

We now come to the surrender of the Friars Minors or Franciscans of Bristol. In this case the document bears no date, but there is very little doubt that it was on the 10th September, 1538, or thereabouts, that the house was given up. This surrender is in slightly different form from the preceding ones. It will be noted that it includes an admission that the King was the supreme head of the Catholick Church of England. This must have been a bitter pill to the unfortunate Friars. In all probability some inducement was offered to them by the King's Commissioner, and finding that resistance was in vain, they thought it expedient to make the best terms they could. The warden did not join in the surrender, and it appears from a note in the inventory of the house (which is the next document transcribed) that he was absent from Bristol. It will be remembered that he was also warden of the convent of Richmond. "Robert Sanderson" appears to have been the name of the warden (Surrender No. 201, Aug. Office).

(COPY SURRENDER OF THE FRANCISCANS.)

"Vn to ow^r most sufferayne Lord Kyng Henri the viijth·
"sup^{r}me hed of the most Catholicke Chyrche of Ynglond
"ĩmedeatly vnder God we the bretherin of ye order of
"saint francis callyd the Graye in bristow wth ow^r hoole

* See p.p. 100-1 as to the Blackfriars conduit.

"assent and cōsent do surrender vp o' house volūtary vn
"to the handis of hys hye maiesť subscribryng o' handis
"psonally.
     " p me frēz Thomā Lewys.
     " Per me frēm Johez Duke.
     " Per me frēm Henricū Carpent'.
     " Per me frēm Johanez M'den.
     " Per me frēm Thomam Lee.
     " Per me frēm Henricū Lawnne."
   (*Exch. Trea. of Rec., Vol. B $\frac{2}{15}$, Fo. 7.*)

(COPY OF THE INVENTORY OF THE HOUSE OF THE BRISTOL FRANCISCANS.)

"THE GREY FREERIS IN BRISTOWE.

"This indenture makith mencyon of all such stuffe of
"the freers mynors in bristowe receyuid by y^e lorde visitor
"vnder the lorde p'uey seale for the Kingis grace, the w^ch
"ys holly delyu'eid to Harry White of Bristowe grocer and
"Willm̄ Popley gentilman to order and saffely kepe the
"same to the Kingis vse, till the Kingis plesure schall be
"further knowen w^t the place and all the appten"nceis.

"THE VESTRE AND QUERE.

" Item ij. peyer of gret brasen candelstickis and ij. peyer of
  "small brasen candelstickis for auters w^t a peyer of
  "timb^r candelstickis.
" Item iij. copis of veluit red blew and blacke.
" Item a cope of damaske.
" Item ij. copis blewe bregis suten and x. pore copis.
" Item vestments for prist decon and subdecon blewe veluit.
" Item for decon and subdecon of red veluit broderyd w^t
  "halfe monys, m^r bowen hath ye vestment.
" Item for prist decon and subdecon of white damaske.

"Item for prist decon and subdecon of sarge w^t lions of golld.
"Item for prist decon and subdecon of bawdkin w^t red
  "closses of veluit.
"Item for prist decon and subdecon of white rosis bore and
  "bestis.
"Item for prist decon and subdecon of bawdkin.
"Item viij. peyer of seingill vestments w^t vj. aubis.
"Item xj. badde auterclotheis.
"Item x. corporas w^t y^r casis ij. pallis and v. serples.
"Item ij. dex clotheis, ij. curteyns for y^e hei aut^r of linig
  "clothe, a banu^r for y^e crosse of sarcenet.
"Item iij. chestis w^{t}owt lockis, ij. cubbordis.
"Item a clothe for y^e hey aut^r in lent season and iij. herse
  "clotheis.

"The Hall.

"Item a tabill ij. trestellys a forme and a cow$^{rt^r}$ borde.

"The Parlar.

"Item scyleid w^t bowdley borde.
"Item a tabill ij. trestellis, ij. cupbordis, a forme and
  "ij. cheiers, ij. carpits, vj. cusseyns.

"The Buttery.

"Item a litill tabill, ij. trestellis, a forme and a cubborde,
  "ij. tabill clotheis.

"The Chamberis.

"Item ij. bedstedis iij. chestis and a cheyer.

"The Kechin.

"Item iij. litill brasse pottis.
"Item iiij. brasen pannys.
"Item a chafer of brasse and ij. laten basens.

"Item iiij. porige discheis of peut^r iij. plateris iij. discheis
 "ij. sawceris.
"Item on long broche and ij. small and a peyer of rackis of
 "iron.
"Item an yron barre w^t iij. hengis and on pothoke.
"Item a treuit and a greidiron w^t a kneding trowe.

"M^d the visitor hathe to ye Kingis vse a crosse dowting
"whether yt be silu^r or no a bande w^t a fote of an horne
"w^t a chales all weing lj. vnc, and y^r be many detters y^t call
"for dettis diūse by tayles diūse by billis but non be payde
"the cause ys ye warden ys not here to know whet^r y^e
"dettis be all oweing or no, but vj. billis appoynted by y^r
"officers to be true dettis the wch billis rest w^t the inventory,
"but non of y^{em} be payde nor non schall be till ye trowthe
"be harde of bothe parteis.

"Also ther ys a litill cofer w^t evidens lefte w^t ye inventory
"and so no peny payde for ye visetors chargis nor other,
"and ther be iij. patents lefte w^t the evidencis.

"p me Harry White.
"p me Willm Popley."

Special reports were made as to the lead belonging to the convents.

Under the heading of "The houses of ffrers lately given "up whiche have any substance of leayde," in Exch. Treas. of Rec., Vol. A $\frac{3}{11}$, F. 4, the following entries appear :—

"The white ffres in Bristowe, oon isle of the church, a
"chapell, and divers grete gutters and conduit."

"The blak freres in Bristowe, two iles in church, iij.
"gutt's bitween the cloyster and the i'batilme't." And at fo. 5, under heading—

"The howses of freres that have no substance of leade,
"save only some of them have small gutts" [gutters].

"The gray freres and the austen freres in Bristowe."

The King, by royal lease, dated 16th March, 1539, granted the Franciscan house and site, together with the gardens and orchards, also the moiety of the prisage of fish, formerly one of the franchises of the Dominicans (which latter moiety was reserved when the King sold the Dominican house and property to Wm. Chester, Esq.), to Jeremy Grene (Green) of Bristol, merchant, for 21 years, "from the last feast of St. Michael the Archangel" (Misc. Books of Court of Aug., Vol. ccxii.—enrolment of leases—Fol. 110ᵇ).

[COPY ROYAL LEASE OF THE FRANCISCAN HOUSE, &c., TO JEREMY GREEN.]

" Hec Indentura fca int excellentissimū principem ɫ dn̄m
" Henricū octauū dei g̃ra Angł ɫ ffranc̃ Regem ɫc̃ ex vna
" parte ɫ Jeronimū Grene de villa Bristoł in Com̃ ville
" Bristoł m̃catorem ex alia parte Testatr q̃d idem dc̃s Rex
" p aduisamentū Consilii Cur̃ Augmentacionū Reuencionū
" Corone sue tradilit concessit ɫ ad firmam dimisit p̃fato
" Jeronimo totam domū ɫ Scitū nup domus dudum fr̃m
" Minoᴣ vulgarit nuncupat leᴣ gray freers infra dc̃am
" villam Bristoł in dc̃o com̃ ville Bristoł modo dissoluɫ
" vnacum Cimitio pom̃tiis gardenis tra ɫ solo infra Scitum
" ɫ pcinctū dc̃e nup domus dudum fr̃m minoᴣ existeñ
" simuleū cursibᴢ ɫ conduct aquarᴣ dict nup domui ptineñ
" siue spectañ adeo plene ɫ integre ac in tam amplis modo
" ɫ forma put nup gardianus ɫ Conuentus eiusdem nup
" domus illa huerunt tenuerunt ɫ gauisi fuerunt. Acceciam
" totam illam firmam prisar' pisciū in Com̃ ville Bristoł
" necnon tot libtar̃ eidem priᴣ pisciū quoquomodo accideñ
" siue em̃geñ quequidm priᴣ pisciū p lras pateñ dc̃i dn̄i
" Regis ex elemosina eiusdem dn̄i Regis nup gardiano ɫ
" Conuentui dc̃e nup domus dudū fr̃m minoᴣ ac nup priori
" ɫ Conuentui dudum domus nup fr̃m p̃dicatoᴣ infra dc̃am

"villam Bristoll simili modo nunc dissolut̃ t eoʒ Successor̃
"concesʒ fuit Exceptis tamen semp t dc̃o dno Regi hered t
"Successoribʒ suis oīnino reseruatis oīnibʒ talibʒ t
"huiusmodi edificus infra scitū dc̃e domus dudum frm
"minoʒ existeñ que dc̃us dñs Rex ibidem p̃sterni t auferri
"mandauit hend tenend t gaudend totū p̃dict̃ Scitū
"Cimitiū pomer̃ t gardina priʃ pisciū ac cet̃a oīnia p̃missa
"cum suis ptiñ Exceptis p̃exceptis p̃fato Jeronimo Grene t
"assigñ suis a festo sc̃i Michis Archi vltimo p̃tito vsqʒ ad
"finem t̃mini t p t̃minu viginti t vnius Annoʒ extunc px̃
"sequeñ t plenar̃ complend Reddend inde annuatim dc̃o
"dno Regi hered t Successoribʒ suis triginta tres solid t
"quatuor denar̃ legalia monete Anglie ad festa Annunciac̄ois
"be marie virginis t sc̃i Michis Archi vel infra vnū Mensem
"post vtrumqʒ festum festoʒ illoʒ ad Cur̃ p̃dc̃am p equales
"porc̄oes soluend durant̃ t̃mino p̃dc̃o Et p'dc̃us Jeronimus
"Grene concedit p p̃sentes q̃d ipe t assigñ sui oīnes necessar̃
"repac̄oes p̃missoʒ de tempore in tempus tociens quociens
"necesse t opportunū fuit bene t sufficient̃ repari sustentari
"t manuteneri fac̃ durant̃ t̃mino p̃dc̃o. In cuius rei
"testimoniū vni pti tc̃ alt̃i vero pti tc̃. Dat̃ apud Westm̃
"decimo sexto die Marcu Anno dc̃i dn Regis tricesimo
"primo.
            "p Consilium Curie p̃dce."

(Copy of the first Half-yearly Account of Jeremy Green.)

"Bristol, } "Account of Jeremy Green, farmer and collector
"A.D. 1539. } "of rents and farms belonging to the late
               "house of the Friars Minors.

        "Accounts for 2^s/4^d for farm of parcel of the
        "site for half a year (of 4^s/8^d per annum) due
        "Michaelmas 1539.

"Also 3ˢ/4ᵈ for farm of a parcel of land called
"The Lower Orchard with little garden demised
"to William Jaye of Bristol, merchant, by
"indenture under the common seal of the late
"Prior and Convent of the said house dated
"15th March 27 Hen. VIII. for the term of 60
"years at 6ˢ/8ᵈ yearly to be paid at Ladyday
"and Michaelmas.

"And 12 pence for farm of Cemetery on the
"west side of the Church of the said house
"abutting on a street called Lewens Mede,
"demised to Thomas White of Bristol, mer-
"chant, at 2ˢ/- yearly.

"And ten shillings for farm of a garden with
"two 'lyme kylnes' and a 'slippe' and a
"little house built thereon situate in a street
"called Lewens Mede demised to Thomas
"Haynes by indenture under the common
"seal of the Prior and Convent 21st June, 25
"Hen. VIII. for 14 years at 20ˢ/- yearly paid
"at Michaelmas and Ladyday.

"Sum (half-year)   16ˢ   8ᵈ

"And 10 shillings for farm of prisage of fish
"within the town of Bristol by letters patent
"under the great seal granted by the King
"12th March, 2 Hen. VIII. to the Friars
"Minors and Preachers within the same town
"now demised to Jerome Green at rent of
"20 shillings.

"Sum (half-year)   10ˢ   0ᵈ

"Sum total   -   26ˢ   8ᵈ."

Subsequently the property of the Franciscans was (inter alia) conveyed to the Corporation of Bristol. In consideration of £1,000 cash and a yearly fee farm rent of £20 the King, by letters patent, dated 2nd May, 1541, granted to the Corporation certain properties, including the Gaunts or House of St. Mark of Billeswicke (now called the Mayor's Chapel), the manors, rectories and churches of Stockland Gaunts and Overstowey, in the County of Somerset, the manors of Gaunt's Eartheott and Lee, in the County of Gloucester, and other valuable estates appertaining to the dissolved house of the Gaunts; the site of the house of the Carmelites or Whitefriars (a portion whereof was afterwards purchased by Sir J. Young, who erected a capital mansion house thereon. This, at a later period, was purchased by Edward Colston for a school, which was subsequently demolished, and upon its site there was erected "Colston "Hall"); a portion of the property of the dissolved Convent of St. Mary Magdalen, situate in Magdalen Lane (now Upper Maudlin Street); and all the property of the Franciscans.* By this conveyance the whole right (*i.e.*, the two moieties) of the prisage of fish coming into Bristol was vested in the Corporation. That body raised a large part of the purchase money in a remarkable manner. Having promised to relieve Bristolians of certain unpopular tolls on goods, the parochial vestries were induced to present it with church plate valued at the then enormous sum of £523 10s. 8d.!

The following references to the Franciscan property in Bristol appear in the "Particulars for Grants," which were drawn up with a view to the preparation of the grant or letters patent, by which the legal estate was transferred to the Mayor and Commonalty of Bristol:—

* The transaction was to date from Michaelmas, 1540.

pcell possessionū t'ūm domus ffr̃m Minoz̧ . . . . . infra villam Bristoll in Com eiusdm ville.	viz.:	Scitus nup domus ffr̃m Minoz̧ Pdcẽ eū terr̃ t possessũ cedm nup domui ptinentĩ.	Vat in		
			Scitũ dc̃e nup domus eũ Cimitor̃ Pomar̃ Gardiñ Terr̃ et Solo infra Scitũ Circuit̃ t p̃cinctũ eiusdm nup Domus existañ sicut Mur̃ lapid̃ includuntur simuleũ Cursub̧ t Conduct̃ Aquaz̧ dict̃ nup domuiptiñ in t'm Amplio mod̃o t forma p̃ut nup prior t confres dc̃e nup domus ea omia huerunt et tenuerunt Duo Jheronimo Grene Reddend inde p Anuũ	xiij˙ iiijᵈ	p anũ clare ijli xiij˙ iiijᵈ	
			Firm̃ vnius pecii Terr̃ vocat le Lymekells dict̃ nup domui ptinent̃ in Tenur̃ Thome Haynes r̃ inde p Annũ	xxˢ	exᵗ p Wiltm	
			Firm̃ Prisaz̧ Piscin infra Com̃ ville Bristoll aut libtat̃ eiusdm Accideñ sine em̃g̃enc̃ nup Prior̃ t̃ Conuent̃ domoz̧ ffr̃m Minoz̧ t p̃dicatoz̧ infra villam p̃dcãm t eoz̧ Successor̃ conceess p fras Patẽn Dn̄i Regis inde eis confect̃ ex Elemosiñ eiusdm dn̄i Regis p Annũ	xxˢ	Berners, Auditorem	

[TRANSLATION.]

			Per annum clear £ s. d.
Part of the possession of the house of Friars Minors without the town of Bristol in the county of the same town, viz.:—	Site of the late house of the Friars Minors aforesaid with lands and possessions pertaining to the same late house.	The site of the said late house with burial ground orchard and garden being the land and soil within the site circuit and precincts of the same late house *as with stone walls they are inclosed*, with courses and conduits of waters pertaining to the said late house in as ample manner and form as the late Prior and brethren of the said late house had and held them all. Sir Jerome Green paying thereof per annum - - - -	13/4
		The farm of one parcel of land called the Lynnekells pertaining to the said late house in the tenure of Thomas Haynes yielding thereof per annum - - - - worth in	20/-
		The farm of the prisage of fish happening or appearing within the county or town of Bristol, or the liberty of the same, granted to the late priors and convents of the houses of friars minors and preachers and their successors within the town aforesaid by letters patent thereof of our lord the King made to them of the alms of the same lord the King per annum	20/-

2 13 4

Examined by Wm. Berners, Auditor.

The property of the late house of the Gray Friars of Bristol was described as follows in the grant to the Mayor and Commonalty of Bristol:—

"All the house and site of the late house, late of the "Minor Brethren, commonly called the Gray Friars, within "our said town of Bristol, now dissolved, and all our "houses, buildings, barns, dovecots, gardens, orchards, burial "places, waters, pools, vivaries, land and soil as well within "as near to, and about the site of seven ambits circum- "ference, and precincts of the said late house of Minor "Brethren, and all waters, water ducts, and water courses* "to the said house of the late Minor Brethren in any way "belonging appertaining running to or flowing from: also our "one parcel of land, called the Lyme Kyln, now or late in "the tenure of Thomas Haynes, in the town of Bristol "aforesaid, to the said late house of the late Minor Brethren, "lately belonging and appertaining, and being parcel of the "possessions thereof: and also all prisage of all and singular "fish within the town, liberties and county of our said "town of Bristol, annually, and from time to time happen- "ing, arising, increasing, or appertaining, which same "prisage of fish lately belonged and appertained to the late "Minor Brethren, and to the late house of Mendicant "Brethren, commonly called the Black Friars, within our "said town of Bristol, now dissolved" (Letters Patent, 6th May, 1541).

[*For information as to the Friars Conduit see ante, pp. 32-3 and 45-53.]

At the same time the property of the Carmelite Friars was conveyed to the Mayor and Commonalty of Bristol, and was described as follows:—"All the house and site of the "late house of the late Carmelite Brethren, commonly "called the White Friars, within our town of Bristol, now

"dissolved; and all the messuage and house, called the
"Hooper's Hall, with the appurtenances, being within the
"site of the said house of the late Carmelite Brethren, and
"all cemeteries, gardens, orchards, land and soil, as well
"within as near to and about the site of seven ambits in
"the circuit and precinct of the same late house of the late
"Carmelite Brethren" (Letters Patent, 6th May, 1541).

[NOTE.—It will be observed that there is no mention of
"waters" or "water ducts" in the description. There can
be no reasonable doubt that the parishioners of St. John
the Baptist had taken over the Friars conduit and water
supply.]

The Carmelite Friars (whose house, according to the
authority of "Speed," was founded A.D. 1267) obtained
their water supply from springs or subterranean streams
situated under land at, or contiguous to, the upper part of
Park Street. The main source of the supply comes from
under **Berkeley** Square or Brandon Hill, but the Friars
may have requisitioned adjacent subterranean supplies in
order to provide against the failure of a particular spring
or stream. Under land, now forming the upper part of
Park Street, about 15 yards from the front of the divisional
wall between Nos. 81 and 83, Park Street (which houses
are on the left hand side going up the street) the Friars
constructed a reservoir or well. There is an arched subway
from this reservoir to a point in front of No. 58, Park
Street (which house is on the right hand side going up) at
which point the archway communicates with the pavement
by a manhole; below this point the subway extends about
15 yards, and then ends at a reservoir or cistern of
considerable dimensions, before reaching the latter the leaden
pipe leaves the subway, through the wall of which it passes
towards **Culver Street**. There are two subways branching

from the main subway, above the point indicated, from which additional supplies of water are obtained from the direction of Brandon Hill. The arched subways and reservoirs are capital examples of early work of the kind.

From Culver Street the pipe is continued across Wells Street to *Crabswell Court, up Frogmore Street to Pipe Lane (so called because the main pipe of this supply was here connected with the Carmelites' cistern). At several points en route cocks are placed in the pipes for the purpose of flushing and repairing when necessary.

The Carmelites granted to the parishioners of St. John the Baptist a feather or branch pipe from the overflow of the cistern in Pipe Lane. The St. John's pipe was carried via St. Augustine's Back (now Colston Street), Host Street, and Christmas Street, to a building erected in the arch just inside the left or eastern side of St. John's Gate, at the junction of Tower Lane and Broad Street. Many years ago the eastern arch of St. John's tower was pierced in order to form a footway for pedestrians, and the water fountain was then transferred to its present position in Nelson Street, which is situated immediately under the Vestry Room of the Church. By Indenture, dated the 2nd day of March, 1865, all the interest of the Feoffees of the parish of St. John the Baptist was transferred to the Town Council of Bristol, and the latter body *is now legally bound to keep the same in repair for the use of the parishioners.* Prior to the date of this conveyance the parishioners had held domain over the whole of the conduit from the date of the surrender of the Carmelites' house, in 1538.

In the month of March, 1893, Mr. C. E. D. Boutflower, Senior Churchwarden, and Mr. W. Bennett, past Church-

---

*The St. Augustine's school is built over the once celebrated Crab's Well.

warden, on behalf of the Vestry of St. John the Baptist, accompanied by Dr. Cook, Analytical Chemist, explored the whole of the subways in Park Street, and the manholes and flushing cocks at various points between Park Street and the Church, and they afterwards reported to the Vestry that the same were found to be in an efficient state. This visit was in consequence of the Sanitary Authority having ordered the supply to be stopped on the ground that the water "showed marked " indications of animal contamination, and was a source of " public danger." Dr. Cook afterwards reported to the Vestry, as the result of his analysis, that "the water is " remarkably free from organic impurity, and may be " safely used for drinking purposes."

. . . . . .

The property of the Black Friars was sold to William Chester, of Bristol, merchant, by royal grant, dated 23rd June, 1540, which conveyed the site of the late house, with buildings, gardens, orchards, churchyard, &c. (containing 6 acres 3 roods) together with 4s. yearly rent of a garden in the site, late in the holding of Richard Abbingdon, and 6s. 8d. rent of a house and garden in the tenure of John Jerdeyne, also a void plot of land outside the wall of the orchard of the house, 73 feet long and 18 feet broad at the west end and 6 feet at the east end, let to Francis Stradlinge, Esq., Jan. 12th, 1537-8, for fourscore years, at the yearly rent of 20d., with the water conduit and all other rights. To be held by the said William Chester by the service of a fief and the rent or tenth of 4s. 2d.— (Palmer's "Friars Preachers or Blackfriars of Bristol").

[NOTE.—The "void plot of land outside the wall of the " orchard of the house" was the place from which the supply of water was obtained, (see will of Nicholas

Excestre, p. 101) and its position points to the probability that the inhabitants of the neighbourhood were allowed to take the water.] The Friars were originally supplied with water by means of a conduit from Paniwell (or Pamwell), afterwards modernized into Pennywell, hence the name of the road (formerly a lane) in the parish of St. Philip (out). The King gave the Friars a license to make and have the conduit on the 18th December, 1232 (Pat. Rolls 17 Hen. III. m. 8), but in the year 1391 they made an exchange with the Mayor and Commonalty of the town, to whom the Friars granted their conduit and the spring called Penywell in consideration that they were to be allowed to have a feather (i.e., a branch pipe) from the town pipe leading from its source at Baptist Mills to the keypipe. The branch pipe issued from the main near "the Bars" (afterwards called Barrs Lane, but now called Barrs Street), and the Friars were thus secured an abundant supply of good water without the expense (to which they had been previously subjected) of keeping the conduit in order, it having been arranged that the town should for ever thereafter bear the expense of keeping the Friars' branch pipe and the town pipe in order (Pat. Rolls 15 Rich. II., p. 1, m. 24).—(Palmer's "Friars Preachers of Bristol.")

In the will of Nicholas Excestre, burgess of Bristol, dated 16th September, 1434, reference is made to "a garden and "close annexed thereto in the suburbs, iux' les Barrez (The "Bars or Barrs Lane) between the little lane 'in qua iacet "Seint Marie Well' and the common gutter by the wall of "the Friars Preachers' orchard and the late close of William "Cary," &c. . . . "extending from the King's way[*] to "the Frome." (Bristol Wills, No. 225.)

---

[*] Now known as "King Street." "Merchant Street" was formerly Mareshalle or Marshall Street (i.e., the place where the Castle troops were marshalled, preparatory to the march to the exercising ground at King's Down).

The property of the Augustinian* Friars was conveyed, with other property belonging to the dissolved religious houses (including property in the county of Kent, &c.) to Maurice Dennys.

(EXTRACT FROM PAT. ROLL 30 HEN. VIII., P. 14, M. 14.)

The King, etc. Know ye that we, for the sum of £536 14s. paid to us by our beloved and faithful servant Maurice Dennys, Esq., have granted to him (inter alia) " **all** " that, site, sept, circuit, and precinct of the late house, some- " time of the Augustinian Friars, within the city or town " of Bristol, with all their rights and appurtenances what- " soever, all the cemetery of the said late house, the close " of pasture within the said site now in the tenure of " Thomas Wynsmore, and all those our houses, buildings, " orchards, gardens, stables, dove-cots, ponds, lands and " soil within the said site, as fully as the last prior or " warden of the said late house sometime of the Augustinian " Friars held the same in right of the said house and in " such ample manner as the said house came to our hands " by reason of the dissolution, suppression or surrender of " the said house. Excepting to us and our heirs all lead " roofs and all the lead on and upon whatsoever buildings " within the said site of the said house, except the lead " gutters and the lead in the windows. To hold the said " site (etc.) to the said Maurice Dennys and his heirs for " ever of us and our heirs in chief by the service of the " 20th part of a knight's fee; he paying yearly to us and " our heirs for the said site and other the premises to the " said house belonging 20d. yearly."

" Witness the King at Westminster 22 March."

The Austin Friars derived their supply of water from a spring called "Ravenswelle," which feeds a reservoir situate

* See ante p.p. 79, 80-3.

near the junction of the roads leading to Bath and Wells respectively. The fountain-head is in a high cliff upon the River Avon. There are at present two entrances to the aqueduct from the rocks on the west side of the river. The pipe may be seen from the river at the point where it emerges from the cavern hewn in the solid rock. There is an old-fashioned wooden door which encloses the passage, and within a few yards from the outside of this door there is a plug inserted in the pipe for flushing purposes. Following the course of the subway the pipe may be traced for about 168 feet when the visitor finds himself again in the open. Here it will be discovered that the excavations made in connection with the recently-constructed loop or goods line from Pile Hill to Brislington have destroyed a portion of the original subway. [We may easily imagine the surprise that must have been caused when, after carrying away a portion of a hill and constructing a cutting of considerable depth, the engineers met with an underground passage high enough for persons to pass through, but this by the way.] The pipe is carried under the railway line, and a doorway recently constructed in the embankment enables us again to pursue our journey through the subway. At a short distance from the newly-constructed entrance will be found the reservoir or tank, which is a very solid and substantial construction, the measurement of which is about 45 feet by 2 feet 6 inches. This is supplied with water from two sources, one of which is reached by a branch subway on the same level, but the source of the main supply can be seen by traversing a branch subway which is about 750 feet(?) in length, at the head of which the springs bubble forth, and the water is conveyed by an aqueduct to the before-mentioned reservoir. The reservoir and subways exist as monuments to the great industry and intelligence of the constructors. Since the excavations for the loop line, the subways have been left open and the pipes are liable to be tampered with. (On the occasion of our recent visit, persons employed by the railway company had lighted a fire in one of the subways.) Pipes have been inserted in the main, and the water is used by the railway company, and an original entrance from the river-side has been blocked with debris. Barratt (p. 553) states that "Sir John de Gourney granted "the ground for an aqueduct 'for the use of the Friars,' and "that Thomas Lyons, Esq., 5 Hen. IV., granted them leave "to carry it through Brandiron Close, otherwise Long "Croft." The friars allowed the parishioners of Temple the right to take the water from a cistern or reservoir, which was placed just outside their house at Temple Gate.

Thomas Blount, burgess and merchant of Bristol, by his will, dated 26th May, 1441, provided that, if the parishioners of Temple "shall hereafter convey, or cause to be conveyed, "the water of a certain conduit now being at the gate "called Temple Gate, from the said conduit, in leaden pipes, "to the Cross of the Temple aforesaid, they are to have "[from testator's effects] 500 pounds of lead for that work."

This will shews that the desirability of bringing the water from Temple Gate to a place more convenient for the parishioners of Temple had been recognised. It is very probable that the testator's wishes were carried into effect shortly after his death. In the year 1508, Stephen Forster, by his will, gave legacies "towards the reparation "of *Temple pipe*, and the conduits of Redcliff, All Saints' and "St. John's in Bristol"—(Bristol Wills, No. 288). The distinction made by the testator between *pipe* and *conduit* tends to prove that, at the date of the will, the pipe only was the property of the parish. After the dissolution of the house of the Austin Friars, in the year 1538, the fountain-head, the conduit, and pipes became the property of the parishioners of Temple. In the will of John Gryffyn, dated 20th April, 1587, the testator refers to "the cundyte "of the said p'ishe of Temple"—(Bristol Wills, No. 406).

There were two feathers in the Temple pipe at one time, supplying Dr. White's Hospital and Temple Vicarage respectively, but the supply has been discontinued for many years. The Rev. W. Hazledine, the present vicar of Temple, states that, in the year 1777, the repair of the conduit was undertaken at considerable expense, and "Neptune," a large leaden statue, which stood in a corner near the tower of Temple Church, was supplied with water. "Neptune," in his new position at the junction of Old Temple Street and Victoria Street, is now supplied with water from the mains of the Bristol Water Co. At one time a portion of the profits of the fair formerly held in Temple parish was appropriated towards the repair of this conduit. The Rev. W. Hazledine, whose kind assistance is acknowledged, states that the supply to Temple parish has been discontinued, and that, in the year 1883, "an "arrangement was made with John Hare & Co., through "whose premises (in Bath Road) the pipe was laid, for the "payment of a yearly sum for the use of the water." It is to be hoped that this valuable supply of water will be restored to the parishioners of Temple. The present condition of the entrances adjacent to the new railway cutting can only be characterised as unsatisfactory. Notwithstanding any statement to the contrary, *there exists a never-failing flow of pure water.* This little work may aptly be brought to a conclusion by respectfully and earnestly appealing to those in whom this conduit is vested to take practical steps for its protection and restoration without delay.

FINIS.

Summary of Contents.

INTRODUCTORY.

	PAGE.
St. Francis, the founder of the order of Friars Minors, his birth, death, and canonization, his first and second General Chapters	v., vi.
Gift of the Church of Portiuncula by Benedictine Monks of Monte Subiaco	vi.
Official recognition by the Pope of Order	vii.
Designation of the Friars of St. Francis	vii.
Colour of Habit*	vii.
Early Franciscans	viii.
Brother Agnellus, the first Provincial Minister of the Order, and eight companions conveyed from France to Dover at the expense of the Benedictine Monks of Fescamp	ix.
Arrival of the Friars in England	viii., ix.
Reception of the Friars by the Benedictine Monks of Canterbury	ix.
Convents of Franciscans at Canterbury, London and Oxford	ix.
Progress of the English Order	ix., x.

CHAPTER I.

BRISTOL FRIARS MINORS.

The Friars Minors of Bristol, their establishment in Bristol—Seyer's references thereto	11, 12
The approximate date of the foundation of the Bristol house	12

* After the Reformation the English Franciscan Friars changed the colour of their habit from gray to brown.

	PAGE.
Visitation at Bristol	13
Death of Brother Agnellus	13
His successor in office	13
Gifts of wood from King Henry III. to the Bristol Friars Minors	14
Declaration by Brother Haymo de Feversham	14
Change of Site of the Bristol Convent	15
Dr. Brewer's reference to Bristol Convent. His conjecture as to the establishment in the suburbs. References thereto and to the Benedictine Monks of St. James's Priory	15-18
Appointment of Reader to Bristol	19
Progress of English Order	19
The Bristol Convent a Chief Custody of the Order	19
Details of Seven Custodies of the Order, A.D. 1399. As to the office of "Warden" or "Guardian," and the Seal of the Bristol Convent	19-21
Stevens' references to Bristol Church and Convent	21, 22
William of Wycestre's measurements of the Friars' Church	22
Ordination in Friars' Church	22
The Site of the Conventual Buildings, Gardens, Orchards, &c.	23-26
Imprisonment of James, Lord Berkeley, in the Bristol Convent, A.D. 1416	26
Outer Boundaries of Friars' Inclosure (see also p.p. 95, 96)	27
Description of Outer Boundaries. Extracts from Itinerarium of William Wycestre	27-32
Remains of Work and Buildings of Bristol Friars. The Friars' Conduit (now All Saints' Conduit, see also p.p. 51-3). Sketches of Remains, Conjectural Plan of Friars' Inclosure	32-41

CHAPTER II.

Bristol Friars Minors.

	PAGE.
Difficulties as to History of Friars Minors, Destruction of their Records, MSS. Books, &c.	43
Preaching of Crusades	44
Thos. de Swinfield, Warden of Bristol A.D. 1282, 1316	45, 46
Thos. de Canynge	46
References to Bristol Friars who held offices in the Order	46, 47
The Conduit of the Bristol Friars (now the All Saints' Conduit)—see also p. 32	47-53
Petition in Norman French from the Bristol Friars to King Edward III. as to Conduit	51
King's License to the Friars to hold Conduit	51-53
Lidiard, John and Joan	51
Grants to Bristol Friars of a Moiety of Prisage of Fish coming into Bristol	53
The other Moiety of the Prisage belonging to the Dominicans or Friars Preachers	53
Grant by King Henry VIII. of Prisage of Fish	53, 54
The Mayor's Prisage of Fish	54, 55
Gifts to Bristol Friars Minors by Will, Deed, &c.	55-64
Gift to Friars of a " Toft "	57, 58
References to Gifts by Will to the four Orders of Friars in Bristol. Examples of Gifts in Kind	64-66

CHAPTER III.

Dissolution of the four Bristol Houses of Mendicant Friars.

Glance at the pre-Reformation History of Bristol. The four Orders of Mendicants, their position with townsmen. References to Gifts to the four Orders by townsmen. Establishment of Chantries, &c.	67, 68

	PAGE.
Payments to the four Orders of Friars by the Bristol Corporation	68, 69
Annual visits of Corporation to the Churches of the Friars Minors and Friars Preachers	69
Friendly feeling of townsmen and Corporation towards Friars	69, 70
Attack on Friars by Lollard Preachers	70, 71
Sermons preached by Latimer in Bristol	71
Sermons preached by Hubberden in reply to Latimer's Sermons	71
Appointment of Commissioners by King as to statements made by Latimer and Hubberden	71
The imposture and conspiracy in the year 1533 by Elizabeth Barton (the "Holy Maid" of Kent)	72
Execution of two Franciscan Friars for participation therein	72
The Wardens of Richmond and Bristol	72
Opposition to King Henry VIII. by Franciscan Friars	72, 73
Dissolution of the Greenwich Convent of Franciscans	73
Dissolution of four Houses of Mendicant Friars in Bristol	74
References to the Bristol House of the Carmelites	74
Surrender thereof	75
Inventory of the contents of the House	76-78
The Friars' Conduit (now St. John the Baptist Conduit) (see also p.p. 98-100)	79
Gift by Carmelite Friars to St. John's parish of a branch Conduit	78, 79
References to the three remaining houses of Mendicants in Bristol	79, 80
Surrender of the Augustinian Friars	80
Inventory of the contents of their house	80-82
References to the Friars' house, gardens, conduit, etc.	82, 83

Contents.

	PAGE.
The Temple Conduit (see also p.p. 102-5)	82, 83
Surrender of the Black Friars	83
Copy inventory of the contents of their house	84-86
References to their house, buildings, conduits, etc.	86-87
Surrender of the Franciscans	87, 88
Copy inventory of their house	88-90
The King's lease of the Franciscans' house, etc. to Jeremy Green	91, 92
The first half-yearly account of Jeremy Green	92, 93
Sale of Franciscan & Carmelite houses and two moieties of prisage of fish by King Henry VIII to the Bristol Corporation	94
Particulars for grant of Franciscan property to the Corporation	95-96
Description of Franciscan and Carmelite properties in the King's letters patent	97-98
The Carmelite Friars' Conduit (now St. John the Baptist Conduit)	98-100
The description of the Black Friars' property in the Royal grant to William Chester of Bristol, merchant	100
The Black Friars' Conduit	100-1
Description of the Augustinian Friars' property in the grant from King Henry VIII to Maurice Dennys, Esq.	102
The Augustinian Friars' Conduit (now the Temple Conduit)	102-5

www.ingramcontent.com/pod-product-compliance
Lightning Source LLC
Chambersburg PA
CBHW030404170426
43202CB00010B/1487